Great Americana

WITHDRAWN

Went to Kansas

Mrs. Miriam (Davis) Colt

Went to Kansas

by Mrs. Miriam (Davis) Colt

READEX MICROPRINT

Foreword

Many of those who went West in search of opportunity were satisfied in their quest. But others, despite every effort, eventually abandoned their newly acquired lands and acknowledged failure by returning to the East. *Went to Kansas*, published in 1862, traces the growing disappointment and the final defeat which one family suffered in the West. In describing her experiences as wife and mother in Kansas, the author, Mrs. Miriam Davis Colt, provides an unusually moving story of courage and heartbreak on the frontier.

For a time Mrs. Colt and her husband had taught school. Then, when Mr. Colt tired of a teaching career, the family moved to a farm near Potsdam, New York. In 1856 Colt determined to sell the farm and to go with his wife and two small children to the territory of Kansas. His goal was a settlement organized by the Vegetarian Settlement Company on the Neosho River in Kansas near Fort Scott. As a practicing vegetarian, Colt was attracted by the idea of living with others who believed as he did. He was excited as well by the fine-sounding economic prospects advertised by the Company.

Mrs. Colt has included in the appendix of her book

the prospectus circulated by the Company, from which it is easy to imagine how attractive the settlement must have appeared. The Company invited people from all parts of the country to purchase shares, in return for which the Company promised to erect mills and other necessary facilities and to provide a common building in which families might take shelter until their own houses were built. The Company announced grandly that "a Hydropathic Establishment, an Agricultural College, a Scientific Institute, a Museum of Curiosities and Mechanic Arts, and Common Schools, will be among the first Institutions of the new settlement." Success seemed certain.

On April 16, 1856, the Colts bade their neighbors goodbye and headed West with all their belongings. But after they had crossed the Little Osage River, Mrs. Colt was beset with disturbing premonitions. When she saw a woman, barefoot, with a sack of corn meal thrown across her shoulder, enter a primitive cabin along their route, she asked herself, "Is that what I have got to come to?" Nor was her morale improved by arrival at the settlement. No buildings had been constructed; everyone was living in tents; and those who had already arrived "tell us they are sorry to see us come to this place."

The most backbreaking work could not overcome the hopelessness of their economic situation. And to this there were threats of Indian attack to be endured, intrusions of poisonous snakes, and the debilitating effects of illness. Unable to hold out any longer, the Colts decided in early September to leave. But greater tragedy awaited. When they reached Booneville, Missouri, on the way back, the Colts' three-year-old son died from an illness contracted in Kansas. Hardly was he buried than Mrs. Colt's husband followed him to the grave. Sustained by sympathetic townspeople, Mrs. Colt kept up her courage and several months later resumed the sad journey East with her daughter.

Mrs. Colt was induced to publish this account of her experiences (based on a diary she had kept) in the hope of adding to the small sum of money she had received from her husband's life insurance. J. Christian Bay furnishes more information about Mrs. Colt in *A Heroine of the Frontier—Miriam Davis Colt in Kansas, 1856* (Cedar Rapids, 1941), pp. 5-9.

WENT TO KANSAS;

BEING

A THRILLING ACCOUNT

OF AN

ILL-FATED EXPEDITION

TO

That Fairy Land, and its Sad Results;

TOGETHER WITH A SKETCH OF THE LIFE OF THE AUTHOR,
AND HOW THE WORLD GOES WITH HER.

BY

MRS. MIRIAM DAVIS COLT.

———— ✦ ————

"There's a Divinity that shapes our ends,
Rough hew them as we will."

———— • ✦ • ————

WATERTOWN:
PRINTED BY L. INGALLS & CO.
1862.

To My Daughter,

MIRIAM LOUISA COLT, WHO HAS STOOD BY MY SIDE WHILE
THE DARK WATERS OF SORROW AND ADVERSITY
HAVE SURGED AROUND ME; AND WHO HAS
BEEN, AND IS A WORLD OF COM-
FORT TO ME,

This Volume is Affectionately Dedicated.

John W. Gorse & Co., Binders.

PREFACE.

IT is with extreme modesty that I present the following pages to be read by other eyes than mine. I do not hand them out expecting that they possess merit enough to interest the million, in these exciting war times; but it is of my friends (those that know me,) and their friends, that I ask patronage, and expect audience.

While in Kansas, I carried a little note-book in my pocket, in which I noted the dates, and the transpirations of each day; so that in writing my sad history, I have carried out the same form, describing the scenes just as they transpired.

What I have written, my friends may rely upon as being the Truth. If it fails of being truth, it is not plus truth but minus truth, on account of my lack of language to describe up to truth.

I have not written, expecting to plate myself over with the purest and most shining of metals, *gold;* neither have I written expecting or wishing to gain "the naphtha lamp of deathless fame;" but *I have written* that I may thereby procure the means to buy my "bread to eat, and wood to warm," and peradventure, redeem my *little home*, which I feel was purchased by the life-blood of my beloved husband!

When common necessities are not supplied, (save by charity,) we cannot wish for riches, or court fame; so that my prayer must be, "Give me this day my daily bread."

My friends will not expect my book to come, bearing the marks of extensive lore; for I have never gathered from the rich halls of science, or reaped from the broad fields of general knowledge; but as I have walked along over earth's uneven highway, now gathering flowers by some silver stream, then clambering over hills and the mountain's rocky cliff, or taking shelter under a spreading leafy tree, or when struggling with the angry waves, have striven to glean.

Neither, while writing, have I been freed from care, or abounded in physical health; I have not hied myself away to a little "sanctum sanctorum," there to get inspired with rich veins of thought, to gush out into profuse descriptive language; but I have sat right here in my little kitchen—have been provider, distributer, mother, mistress of the house to receive and entertain all who might chance to come, (and the number has not been small;) have been housekeeper, "chief butler and baker," laundress, sewing girl, chore boy, sick nurse, and invalid besides; for as often as once in three weeks (during the six months I have been writing,) I have been confined to my bed for three successive days, with a dreadful sick and nervous headache.

I must ask the kind indulgence of my friends, knowing that my writing can be subjected to criticisms; but under the circumstances, driven by necessity, with a mountain's weight of inability resting upon me, if others can do more and better, I will give them God's speed.

If I awaken sympathy for the afflicted of earth, by patronage procure my heart's desire, and give courage to the suffering to "bear up awhile beneath life's pressures," until "one unbounded spring encircle all," then my labor has not been in vain.

MIRIAM D. COLT.

WEST STOCKHOLM, St. Lawrence
    Co., N. Y., July 1, 1862.

TABLE OF CONTENTS.

CHAPTER I.

Anticipations and preparations — Vegetarian Co.,— H. S. Clubb's circular—Going to Kansas—Preparations for journey—Letter from H. S. Clubb—Decision—Packing and starting.

CHAPTER II.

Our journey—Bid farewell to friends—Detained at Watertown—Stop at Buffalo—Take Lake Shore route for Cleveland.—Stop at Indianapolis—Arrive at St. Louis—Go on board steamer for Kansas City—"The call to Kansas"—Journey into the territory—Fording rivers—Camping—Arrive at destination.

CHAPTER III.

Disappointments and discomforts—Find no mills—No place of shelter—"The centre Octagon"—Improve it—Our dormitory—Rainy season—Simple food—Manner of cooking—Hope revived—Expect a saw mill—Company leave—Receive calls—Washing—Baking—Take claims—Build cabins.

CHAPTER IV.

Ploughing and planting—A busy time—Ploughing by moonlight—Mrs. Herriman sick—Visit her, carry flowers—Climate of Kansas—Ramble in the bottom lands—The Neosho—Vines and berry bushes—Indians, dress and wild nature—Go with husband to plant corn—A spot selected for cabin—Don the Bloomers—Flowers—A novel picture—Church at Mr. Clubb's—The eager cattle—Spider wart—Thunder storm—The Indians gone on a hunt—Presentiments—Plough broken—Mr. Herriman leaves the Territory—Sabre gone—Sambo day—Tune for Flowers—Visit to the ruined wigwams—Indian utensils—Purslain plant.

CHAPTER V.

The unsettled state of the Territory—Northern invasion—What Willie said—Mr. Buxton—No papers—The city of Lawrence destroyed—Osawatomie sacked—Mob threaten to come here—Trunks locked—I am made Treasurer—May Heaven save us—Air—Bugbear—Straw ticks filled with prairie grass—Musquetoes—Fencing cornfields—H. S. Clubb's house—Soft stone for building—Limestone—Coal—Baking Days—White bread—Writing home—Letter from St. Louis—Dried apple and berries—Grasshoppers—Evening prim roses—Big creek—Whippoorwill—Frogs.

CHAPTER VI.

The fever and ague has surely come—Mother, Lydia, Mema, Mr. V. and wife all sick—Mr. V. intends leaving the Territory—I am taken sick also—Husband concludes to leave—Husband washes—We cook for journey—The water failing—Father hunts for water—Doomed to disappointment—Father takes mother and sister L., and goes to Indian house—Mr. V. and wife leave for Kansas City—What shall we do?—Submit to paternality—H. S. Clubb sick—Leaves the settlement—Sick at Mr. Adams'—Stewart's—Broadbent's—The Oliver brothers leave—Willie taken sick—Unhappy Fourth—Husband returns from cornfield sick—Thunder storm—We go to Indian house—Spring of cold water—Husband goes to Mr. Stewart's, is sick with fever and ague—All sick but father and myself—Father draws water.

CHAPTER VII.

All sick but myself—Mr. Buxton here—Writing home—Sick ones scattered about—Three months from Northern home—Go to settlement—Borrow a sieve—Mr. Stewart and wife visit us—Buxton takes sick and goes home—I am nurse and maid—Take care of oxen, cow and calf—Bring water—Attend to the sick—Mourning dove—Charnel house of red men's bones—Indian burial—Snakes—Mysterious personage—Take sick ones out to ride—Drive oxen—Storing water to wash—Wolves—Husband's birth-day—Oxen run away—Go for them—Lose my way, but find lovely dells and grain fields—Go again for oxen—See Mr. Stewart—Ride home—Father Broadbent's visit—Prayer.

CHAPTER VIII.

Indians return from hunt—Timely warning—Critical hour— My proposal—Take leave of family—Kiss my Willie again— Start off—Walked, run or flew—Fear of being seized by Indians —At the cornfields by sundown—Osage's superstition—Hurry on for fear of darkness and getting lost—Reach Mr. Adams'— Make known our danger—Mr. Adams makes ready men and teams—Mr. Stewart and Broadbent start with me—Thunder storm—Woolen quilt—Confused and bewildered—The oxen's instinct—The moon—Scattering trees—The cry of "a light," "a house,"—Thanks to Heaven—Embrace my family—Husband's anxiety—The men asleep—No sleep for me—The dawn of day— Bid a glad adieu to Indian house—Sweet corn and squashes— Arrive at settlement—Condition of cabin—"Puncheons" and heater, beds and trunks take their former place—Thanksgivings and rejoicings.

CHAPTER IX.

Life at the settlement again—A letter from Mrs. V.—Another terrific thunder storm—A walk of four miles for spring water— The Indians pass and re-pass, going to Cofuchigue with dried buffalo meat and tallow—Their hungry dogs—Buy buffalo meat —Green corn and squashes in abundance—Family some better —Mr. V.'s cornfield—Mr. V.'s flowers and tomatoes—My dream —Hot days—Mr. Adams, wife and child, and young men sick— Mr. Stewart's family sick—We go to see Mr. Clubb—A shower on our return—A long, drizzling rain—bring water through the wet grass—Chase after cow—Husband tries to persuade father again to leave the Territory, but all in vain; he must stay to sell land—Indians destroying our corn—Steal the melons—Oxen cannot be found—Sunday morn—Sister L. and Mema go with me for water—White crows—Quails—Another letter from Mrs. V.—Intend to leave the country—Washing, and white clothes—

Willie afraid the Indians will carry off his mamma—Trunks packed, and cooking done for our journey—Mr. Breadbent sick —Indian amenities—Our family better—Wagon sold—Agree with Mr. Morris to take us out of the Territory—Disappointed again—My husband's dream—He divides funds—Spike of flowers—Another chance to go—Make arrangements with Healy— The big melon.

CHAPTER X.

Our journey from the Neosho, &c.—View the journey before me—Camp at Conreal's—Pass the Catholic Mission—Camp on Cow creek—Lame ox—Cooking by camp fire—Bad water—Rumors of war—Reach marks of civilization—Driver obstinate— Husband stays in a house—A rainy night and morning—Look in at Mr. Decker's—Families propose a rest—Our ruffian driver demands our blood or our money—The scene overcomes my husband—He has a chill—Gives the crazy driver a little—He threatens to leave us by the side of the road—Find a place in a house for husband—Sleep with my children in the wagon—Insulted by drunken driver—He is persuaded to take us on a few miles—We stop at Carthage, Jasper Co., Mo.—Find a friend in one Mr. Wells—Husband and children sick some—Stop one week with Mr. Wells—Leave for Booneville, Mo.—Mr. Wheeler sick—Leave him at Mellville—Willie taken sick with dysentery —Hold him on pillows all day—Watch with him all night—We travel on—Arrive at Booneville—Stop at Bullock's hotel—Mema sick—Willie very sick—Mema better—I still watch with trembling.

CHAPTER XI.

Willie's death—Bury him in the city burying ground, a lovely, retired spot—Receive much sympathy from stranger friends— Pack trunks to journey—Purchase grave stones for Willie, (pay with my own clothes,) marked, *Willie, the little stranger*—Husband tries to sell gold watch—My dream—Husband taken sick See the stones placed at Willie's grave—Call Dr. McCutchen— Friends try to comfort me with hope of husband's recovery—My heart is sorrowful—husband no better—Friends kind—Hus-

band's advice in case of his death—My husband's death and
burial—We go to Capt. Walter's pleasant home—A letter from
St. Louis states that my goods are in Kansas City—I must not
grieve, but up and attend to business—Much sympathy, and administering to necessities—The county fair, but no desire to go—
Write a long letter in regard to goods—Headache—My husband's clothes sold at auction—The avails used to purchase him
gravestones—A pleasant Sabbath—The negro servants—Notice
of husband's death in the paper—Go to the burying ground to
see husband's gravestones set—Take a last farewell—Have papers made out to send to Insurance Co.—Take leave of my kind
stranger friends.

CHAPTER XII.

Step out on the sea of life alone—Journey from Boonville to
Jackson, Mich.—Meet with a warm reception from friends—Ride
about the city — Visit to the state prison — Visit a brother in
Parma—Mema sick—Return to Jackson—Sad news—Father
Colt's death and burial in Kansas—Mother Colt and sister L.
start for the State of New York—They arrive in Stockholm, N.
Y.—Mother Colt's death the 4th of November—Mema very sick
with the chills—Hear O. S. Fowler lecture on Phrenology—
Holidays in Jackson—Sister Lydia's death—Journey to Owassa,
Mich.—Stop one night in Lansing—Stay one week in Bingham
—Pass through thrifty towns—Owassa (bright spot)—Receive
letters from friends—Visiting with friends—Letters from the
Insurance Co.—Write to Montreal—Policy lost—Write to Hartford—Give bonds—Receive insurance money—Invest it—Leave
Owassa for Jackson, on the cars—Visit and bid farewell to
friends—Start for New York—Visit Niagara Falls—Sick at Syracuse—Arrive at Potsdam—In West Stockholm—Purchase a
little land to make a home—Visit, and receive letters from
friends—My goods arrive—My home ready—Move into it—Barn
and henery built—The widow's home and heart.

CHAPTER XIII.

My early life—My pedigree — My father's character—My

mother—My place of nativity—Entrance upon this life—A puny childhood—Fifteen years of age before I had books or health to study—Joined the church before I was fourteen—My desire to dress well—Aspirations for knowledge—Kept house for a brother —Death of a little brother—Attended school winters—Taught school—Was successful—My minister's approval—Journey to St. Lawrence co.—My stay in Fort Covington—A pleasant time My father's moving to Parishville—Our pleasant home—My teaching and going to school—My marriage—Mema's birth—My life in the city, and love of the same—Our removal to the country—Boarding and visiting—Birth of my Willie—Living on a farm—Genealogy of the Colt family—My husband's birth-place —Removal to New York—His occupation and education.

CHAPTER XIV.

How the world goes with me—"Only waiting"—My intentions of improving my little home—Setting trees and cultivating flowers—My interest not paid—My effort for a livelihood—Called to mourn—My brother sells and leaves—Called to mourn again —Remembered by my Booneville friends—Adversity still reigns —The farm sold on which my security rested—I am called to pay my little debts—My health poor—The cold winter—My neighbors get me wood—My nephew sends a little money—Mema's poetry—Messages from my husband—My husband's whisper—The war—My neighbors—Fitting Mema to take care of herself—The poultry business—Poverty still gapes upon us— Relief from Montreal friends—Still try to improve our home— Praise God, and ask for grace.

CHAPTER I.

"Bring the sickle, speed the plough,
  Turn the ready sail;
Freedom is the noblest pay
  For the true man's. toil.
Ho! brothers! come brothers!
  Hasten all with me,
We'll sing upon the hunter's plain
  A song of liberty."

JAN. 5TH, 1856.—We are going to Kansas. The Vegetarian Company that has been forming for many months, has finally organized, formed its constitution, elected its directors, and is making all necessary preparations for the spring settlement.

The directors of said Company are "Charles H. DeWolf, President; John McLaurin, Treasurer; Henry S. Clubb, Secretary."*

H. S. Clubb says in his circular: In September last, Dr. John McLaurin, as one of the directors, proceeded to explore Kansas Territory, and after

---

*Its origin, site, octagon plan of settlement, names of members and constitution may be found in the appendix.

spending several weeks in traveling along the Kansas, Osage and other rivers, he came to the conclusion that a fine site on the Neosho river, between latitude 38 deg. and the boundary line of the Osage Indian lands, and between 18 and 19 deg. longitude west from Washington, would be the best location for the Vegetarian Settlement. He accordingly took possession of a claim, comprising excellent water privileges. The river at this part is very rapid, and for ten months in the year the water is sufficiently abundant to make it serviceable for mill-power. It is free from any bad taste and is very soft. There is sufficient amount of timber to serve the purposes of settlers until additional timber can be grown. Coal, lime-stone, and sand-stone, suitable for grindstones, etc., and abundant springs of pure water are interspersed throughout a fine rolling prairie, and the land comprises excellent vegetable mould, loam, etc., to a great depth, with a gravelly and in some instances rocky substratum. The distance from Fort Scott is about thirty miles, and from the Missouri border thirty-eight miles. It will be seen, by reference to the map of *American Railway Guide*, that a railroad is projected which will cross the Neosho river a little below the spot above indicated. The land is open to pre-emption five miles wide north and south, and to an unlimited extent east and west. The scenery is beautiful, and the surface undulating like the waves of the ocean subsiding after a storm.

The banks of the river are from fifteen to thirty

feet high, so that a mill-dam can be easily constructed without causing an overflow.

Altogether it does not appear that a more suitable
site could be found for the purposes of the company.

We now present the plan of action by which we
propose to commence the Settlement, and we confi-
dently ask for the active co-operation of every member as soon as is consistent with his or her conven-
ience.

PLAN OF OPERATION.

1. To raise a fund for the purchase of a saw-mill,
a grist-mill, and provisions, seeds, plants, grain, tents,
etc., for the first settlers, and for the erection of a
boarding-house, in which persons may reside without
risk to health, until their own houses can be erected.

2. The money to be raised by an assessment of 10
per cent. on the capital subscribed, or of fifty cents
per share, and by loans.

3. The property to be held by the directors, as
trustees of the company, until the members shall
meet in quorum and appoint their own officers.

4. The payment of fifty cents per share from each
shareholder to be due on the 1st of Jan., 1856. But
all payments received within the month of January,
1856, will be considered as regular.

5. Members will be charged interest at the rate of
one per cent. per month, commencing with January
1st, 1856, for any amount due at that date, if not

paid within the said month. The interest to continue until such amount shall be paid.

6. Loans to the company paid within the month of January will bear interest from the first of said month, at the rate of one per cent. per month.

7. Every member is requested to communicate to the Secretary within the month of January, in relation to the following particulars:

I. The amount of money the member pays within the month.

II. Whether the member intends to go to Kansas in February and assist in preparing for the larger number who will be on the ground in April or May.

III. How many persons will accompany the member, with the name, age and occupation, etc., of each person, and relationship to the member, if any. Also the same particulars in regard to persons who are expected to follow when the member has established a home in the Settlement.

IV. The name, age, address, occupation and amount of capital of the member making said return.

8. All money to be sent addressed Henry S. Clubb, care of Fowler & Wells, 308 Broadway, New York city, by drafts on New York houses, payable only to the 'order of Henry S. Clubb.'

9. It is expected that the plan of the Settlement will be completed, and the lots ready for distribution on the first day of May, 1856, when it is requested that all members of the company be present, either personally or by duly appointed agents

10. Members who are present at the Settlement prior to the first of May, will be employed by the company according to article VIII of the constitution, in preparing the Settlement for occupation. Improvements thus made will accrue to the benefit of the whole company.

11. All claims taken up by members previous to the first of May, 1856, will be understood, in honor, as subject to the adjustment to take place on that day; but all improvements made by individuals on such claims will be paid for by the company, according to a fair valuation, either in cash or stock, whenever said claims are required in general distribution to be donated to other members. The appraisers to be elected by the members of the company in the same way as other officers.

12. When a sufficient sum of money shall have been received, the directors will proceed to make preparations for early spring emigration, and such members as intend going first will be communicated with as to the best route and where to meet the directors.

This is the plan of action which we are prepared in good faith to carry out in accordance with the provisions of the constitution, which have already received the approval of the members. We need not remind you that the profits and advantages which may be realized will accrue to all on the mutual principle, and that the scrip given in exchange for the payments will be exchangeable at the Settlement

2

for provisions, use of teams, lumber and other valuable considerations, rendering said scrip equal to bank notes as currency in the Settlement. The success of the undertaking must now depend upon the promptness with which this circular is responded to by each member and by friends. Those who can spare more than fifty cents on each share are requested to send loans, and those who cannot pay the full interest are requested to send as much as they can spare, so that ample provision can be made for the early settlers.

Mechanics, lumbermen, carpenters, iron-workers and laborers will be sure of good employment in the Settlement as early as weather will permit operations to commence in the Spring of 1856, and they can, by their labor, become stockholders in the company.

All whose labor shall exceed in value the amount due on their shares, will be paid interest for any amount they may loan the company, in the same way as capitalists.

All shareholders who shall pay up the first and second installments in or before the month of January, 1856, will be entitled to be regarded as among the founders of the Settlement; their names will be applied to the avenues or streets adjoining their respective farms, as far as practicable, and they will be entitled, according to the date of receipts for the first installment of ten cents per share, to preference in the distribution of lots in May, 1856.

The directors do not pledge themselves to sell any

shares for as low as $5 per share after January 31st, 1856, as, the location being favorable, there is no doubt but shares will rise rapidly in price. It is not improbable that after January 31st, shares will be raised to double their present price.

Members will be careful not to communicate the contents of this circular to any but known and trust-worthy friends of the enterprise, as the precise location ought not to be publicly known, until all the claims required by the company are taken.

We have thus far executed the trust reposed in us, and we pledge ourselves to a further faithful per-formance of our duties, as directors, and to devote our capital and personal attention to the company and its best interests to the full extent of our ability and judgment. It is a work in which we all feel deeply and equally interested, believing that it is calculated to form a nucleus of true reforms in the centre of our republic, such as must exercise an un-precedented influence for good in the future.

We call upon you as members and friends, to each and all do your part, and to remember that when we faithfully perform our duty we can rely on the all-sustaining hand of *Providence* to prosper our under-taking. The first effort is the most important one in securing the permanent success of the Settlement, and all who are friendly to the undertaking are re-spectfully solicited to render their aid *at the time specified*, and not to wait and see if we succeed, be-fore they come forward with their assistance. **We** ask no magnanimous liberality, but a generous business co-operation of capital and labor, with a view to mutual interest and the general good of the cause.

We have been frequently asked how can the company be assisted by persons who cannot actively unite with us? We reply to every such inquirer: Find some trustworthy, enterprising young man, and purchase for him shares in the company, on condition that the loan shall be returned when the concern shall enable him to refund.

Let printing presses, machine shops, sawing, planing and grist mills be established by members; let sash factories, door factories and foundries be commenced; let coal mines, stone quarries and brick yards, with all the appliances of machinery, be started; and above all, let the land be cultivated under the advantages by mutual aid, of capital, machinery and skill; let orchards be planted and the various farm crops pursued in proper rotation, and with the growing demand of this new territory, and connecting with the various channels of commerce, throwing the whole United States open as a market for its productions, there is good reason to believe that the Settlement will be in a most flourishing condition in the course of a few quickly passing, because busily occupied, years, and the lands now obtainable at the minimum government price of $1 25 per acre, will be worth from $25 to $50 and even $100 per acre; while on the Octagon plan of settlement, every acre will be convertible into suitable building sites, the value of which cannot now be estimated.

No one can examine our list of members without being convinced that we have the elements of such a Settlement already belonging to our company. The brand of our settlement must ere long become a guarantee throughout the country of genuine and wholesome articles of diet.

The advantages to families of having their children educated away from the ordinary incentives to vice, vicious company, vicious habits of eating and drinking, and other contaminations of old cities, must render the Vegetarian Settlement a most desirable place of residence to all whose tastes are averse to those habits of gross indulgence which are degrading to mankind.

Signed by the Directors,

CHAS. H. DE WOLFE,
JOHN McLAUREN,
HENRY S. CLUBB.

New York City, Dec. 1st, 1855.

We can have, I think, good faith to believe, that our directors will fulfill on their part; and we, as settlers of a new country, by going in a company will escape the hardships attendant on families going in singly, and at once find ourselves surrounded by improving society in a young and flourishing city. It will be better for ourselves pecuniarily, and better in the future for our children.

My husband has long been a practical vegetarian, and we expect much from living in such a genial clime, where fruit is so quickly grown, and with people whose tastes and habits will coincide with our own.

JAN. 15TH.—We are making every necessary preparation for our journey, and our home in Kansas. My husband has sold his farm, purchased shares in the company, sent his money as directed by H. S. Clubb, and will first go alone or will take his family right along, as he makes up his mind will be for our happiness, comfort and health. My husband is quite satisfied from what he can glean from the Tribune and other sources, that Kansas will soon be left to her quiet, and come in as a free State—so we have little fear about the "Border Ruffian Invasions," etc. I am very busy in repairing all of our clothing, looking over bags of pieces, tearing off and reducing down, bringing everything into as small a compass as possible, so that we shall have no unnecessary baggage. Am making a good many carpet rags for some of my friends that I leave here in Stockholm.

FEB. 4TH.—We have been to Potsdam, the distance of 14 miles, purchased clothing sufficient to last us two or three years. Found the snow very deep and terribly drifted, rendering the roads some of the way impassable, obliging us to drive through people's door-yards, barn-yards, out into the fields, over fences, gates and stone walls. Our sleigh capsized only once, leaving us to scrabble up and replace

ourselves all snugly again in the sleigh to drive on.
Took our two children, visited our friends in Potsdam and others on the way going and coming. On
the whole had quite a gay time.

MARCH 15TH.—Have had two sewing bees; one
for the old ladies, and one for the young—"united
pleasure with business"—my friends have visited me
for the last time—also have helped me along with
my sewing.

MARCH 20TH.—Am getting my sewing pretty well
done up, and the bright days of spring-tide, that are
now wearing the deep and drifted snow away, call
our thoughts away to the sunny South, causing us
to anticipate much in our Southern home. Even
little Willie talks about his "Indian pony" and
"little wagon" he is going to have, and how he shall
give mamma a ride on the prairies and pick the little
wild apples.

APRIL 2D.—My husband has received a letter from
Henry S. Clubb, which brings him to the conclusion
to take his family along with him. So we are not
to be left behind. I could not bear the thought of
having him go without us. H. S. Clubb writes as
follows:

"ST. LOUIS, March 26th, 1856.

W. H. COLT—Dear Sir: It is intended to proceed
so as to make the distribution of lots according to

the notice given in December last, and see nothing
to prevent our doing so.   Eighteen of our party are
gone on to the territory, and I remain here to escort
another party the first week in April.   Watson
Stewart will leave Lafayette, Indiana, on the 20th
of April, escort a third party, intending to be at the
Settlement on the first of May.   Write him, and arrange to meet him with your family along with you,
as there will be proper provision for a family at that
time, and there would be a great expense incurred in
your coming back for them, and nothing saved.
Come with as little baggage as possible.   Mr. Young,
of Poplar Ridge, and Miss Smith, of Marcellus, both
from New York State, are here.   I know of no other
members near you just now.   *   *   *

         Faithfully,   HENRY S. CLUBB.

APRIL 10TH.—We are all in confusion—beds taken
down, furniture sold that we do not want to carry,
the rest boxed up—here are our trunks all packed;
and we find ourselves *all so packed up* that we cannot take another meal of victuals here in our house.
Surely we are on the eve of starting for Kansas.
We shall stay at Mr. Willis' to-night, and in the
morning George Willis will take me and the children
to my brother's, the distance of seven miles, where
we shall visit my mother, while my husband is help-
ing his father to finish up their packing.   My Willie
boy's order has been very much disturbed by the
confusion that has been in the house for a few days

past; he has said many times, "*Wish Willie was in Kansas.*"

After living in Stockholm two years I find that my sympathies and the warm feelings that live in my heart for my friends and neighbors are not as easily gathered up and boxed as are our goods; and when I am far away, shall feel that the cords of friendship and love are still clinging to my old friends.

May Heaven grant that ours may be a prosperous journey—and may we find in that southern clime all we anticipate to make us a comfortable and pleasant *home.*

APRIL 15TH.—Have been here in West Stockholm, at my brother's, since Friday last. Have visited mother very hard, for, in all probability, it is the last visit we shall have until we meet *where parting never comes*—believe we have said everything we can think of to say.

My husband has come, says he has got the old people started for Potsdam to be ready for the stage early in the morning—he is going right along on foot, so as to get into the bank to get some money before it closes. My brother will take me and the children out this evening.

CHAPTER II.

All our good-byes have been spoken,—hands shaken,—kisses pressed in token of love and friendship
that will burn in hearts like ours, wheree'er we turn.

APRIL 16TH.—ANTWERP, N. Y.—Bade our friends
good-bye, in Potsdam, this morning, at the early
hour of two o'clock. Have ridden forty miles in a
stage-coach, over very rough roads. In some places
we found the snow four and five feet deep—we were
obliged to get out and walk some distance. The
men had to work hard to keep the stage right side
up. We found ourselves very much crowded; even
our own family was enough to fill one stage, there
being seven of us, father, mother and sister Lydia
Colt, my husband, self and two children. We have
now arrived safely in this place, but a few minutes
too late for the five o'clock train; we saw the train
start out just as we were coming in. We are all
very tired, and glad to lay ourselves down to rest.

APRIL 17TH.—STANWIX HALL, ROME.—We took

a freight train this morning, at nine o'clock, for Watertown; arrived there about noon; were in hopes to find a passenger train going out at twelve o'clock, but were disappointed. A dark, rainy day. I need not say how long the hours seemed, nor how tired the children got, nor how many times Willie asked me, "How long before the old iron bonny will come?"

We tried to amuse ourselves by reading the advertisements of different routes and the faces of strangers, who, like us, were waiting for the five o'clock train; but it is exceeding hard to amuse one's self while waiting for the cars.

We find ourselves well cared for here in this splendid, neat, and quiet hotel after our weary day of waiting.

APRIL 18TH.—Here we are, at the close of another day, in Buffalo. Have journeyed through a most beautiful country to-day. This Western New York is not to be equalled in this northern country for beauty of scenery, or fertility of soil. My husband wishes to take very good care of us all, particularly the old people; so we have left the cars and are resting in this nice hotel, "The Stranger's Home." My head aches so hard, that I care but little where I am, if I can only find a place to be quiet, and rest my poor head.

APRIL 20TH.—INDIANAPOLIS, IND.—Am resting this

pleasant Sabbath day, after being on the cars twenty-
four hours. From Buffalo, took the Lake Shore
route to Cleveland, Ohio, from thence to this place.
Lake Erie looked blue and boundless, and we could
see the white sails in the distance. Have passed
beautiful green fields of wheat, and fine tall trees all
in leaf; have seen gardens being made, and wild
flowers blooming. Here is an apple tree close by
the window, almost in full blossom—surely we are
moving southward! southward! How quick the
transition from winter to spring. In four days have
travelled from snow banks and ice-bound streams, to
green fields, leafy woods, smiling flowers, and the
merry notes of birds.

Willie and his papa have been visiting the cemetery. Willie brought a sprig of cedar to his mamma.
Mema is contented if she can get a book. This hotel is full of people—all strange faces—truly we are
among strangers, bound for a new home. This Indianapolis is a beautiful place. The people are coming from church. The day seems long.

APRIL 22D.—Have been on the cars again since
yesterday morning. Last night was a lovely moon-
lit night—a night of thought, as we sped almost
with lightning speed, along in the moonlight, past
the rail fences.

The sun is just rising in the east, casting his gold-
en rays all over this beautiful country, with its trees
in leaf. Here we come into Illinois Town; right

before us the great Mississippi, "the father of waters," while just over, the city of St. Louis, in all its compactness, rises step by step, a city on a hill side, almost enveloped in smoke. Truly this has been called "a city of smoke."

Found ourselves in this miserable hotel before we knew it. Miserable fare—herring boiled with cabbage—miserable, dirty beds, and an odor pervading the house that is not at all agreeable. Mistress gone.

APRIL 23D.—On board steamer "Cataract," bound for Kansas City. Our company that we expected to meet here are all on board. They seem to be very fine people.

APRIL 24TH.—A hot summer day. The men of our company are out in the city, purchasing wagons and farming implements, to take along on the steamer up to Kansas City.

Am amusing myself in viewing this wonderful river. Here is a floating city of steamboats; they lie wedged in so close to each other, that it is a wonder to me how they are ever going to start out, even when they want to. Still I see them go out and come in, above and below, as difficult as it looks. If one should take fire, I am sure we should all be burned. The levee is piled almost mountain high with merchandise, enough, I should think, to supply all America. The negroes are loading and unloading it on to and off from the steamers all the time.

APRIL 25TH.—The "Cataract" has liberated herself from the mass of steamers. Am viewing the city as we move along up the river· One dark column of smoke rises and curls over her house-tops, domes and spires.

Twenty-five miles up the river. Now enter the dark, muddy waters of the Missouri; large trees have been washed from its banks during high water, and lie along in its bed, with their limbs extended, always ready to "snag" the steamers as they ply up the river. The channel of the river, they say, is continually changing, so that it requires much tact and experience to be a pilot on the steamers.

APRIL 26TH.—Was kept awake most all night; it seemed as though we were on a sand-bar once in five minutes; then how the steamer would puff and wheeze to liberate herself.

A lovely morning. What beautiful, grand moving scenery—high bluffs, sloping woodlands, green fields, blooming flowers, little cottages, fruit trees all in blossom, nestling in between the craggy cliffs. Here is the town of Herman, noted for its wine. These cliffs and bluffs are wild and grand in the extreme; some are 200 feet high, perpendicular and smooth; they remind one of the descriptions of eastern castles, and you can easily imagine that the chisel marks are to be seen on the massive walls.

The evening is dark; the thunder is roaring, the lightning flashing, and the rain comes in torrents.

Here at Jefferson City, have more of our company come on board. Good news from our southern home—our company happy and hopeful.

APRIL 27TH.—Sunday. Have had preaching on board the Cataract—good attention. These 200 passengers all eat at the same table three times a day, are very friendly, and seem like one large family.

Have just passed a beautiful little place in between the cliffs. Now we come to the pretty town of Booneville, situated on a bluff. An old woman comes on board to sell apples; Oh! she tarries too long, the plank is taken up, and she is left on board. Is making a great fuss; she is brought along three or four miles, and is being set off on a bluff.

APRIL 28TH.—The steamer struck a "snag" last night; gave us a terrible jar; tore off a part of the kitchen; ladies much frightened. Willie is not very well; the water is bad; it affects all strangers.

A lovely eve. We are going on up the river. All seem happy. Some of our company are out on the guards, singing the following song:

CALL TO KANSAS.—Air: " *Nelly Bly.*"

BY LUCY LARCOM.

Yeomen strong, hither throng—
   Nature's honest men—
We will make the wilderness
   Bud and bloom again.
Bring the sickle, speed the plough,
   Turn the ready soil;
Freedom is the noblest pay
   For the true man's toil.
      Ho, brothers! come brothers!
       Hasten all with me,
       We'll sing, upon the Kansas plains,
       The song of liberty.

Father haste! o'er the waste
   Lies a pleasant land;
There your fire-side altar-stones
   Fixed in truth shall stand;
There your sons, brave and good,
   Shall to freemen grow,
Clad in tripple mail of right,
   Wrong to overthrow.
      Ho, brothers! come brothers!
       Hasten all with me,
       We'll sing, upon the Kansas plains,
       A song of liberty!

Mother come—here's a home
   In the waiting West—
Bring the seeds of love and truth,
   You who sow them best;
Faithful hearts, holy prayers,
   Keep from taint the air;

Soil a mother's tears have wet,
  Golden crops shall bear.
    Come mother, fond mother,
      List, we call to thee,
    We'll sing, etc.

Brothers brave, stem the wave,
  Firm the prairie tread;
Up the dark Missouri flood
  Be your canvas spread.
Sister true, join us too,
  Where the Kansas flows;
Let the Northern lily bloom
  With the Southern rose.
    Brave brother, true sister,
      List, we call to thee:
    We'll sing, etc.

One and all, hear our call
  Echo through the land—
Aid us with a willing heart
  And a strong right hand—
Feed the spark the pilgrims **struck**
  On old Plymouth Rock;
To the watch-fires of the free
  Millions glad shall flock.
    Ho, brothers! come brothers!
      Hasten all with me,
    We'll sing upon the Kansas plains,
    A song of liberty.

APRIL 29TH.—Rainy and cold; fire very comfortable. These steamers have been truly called "floating palaces." The waiters are just beginning to lay

3

the table for dinner; I like to watch them, to see with what order and precision everything is brought on; such a variety of meats and fish, and all kept smoking hot on the table. Then comes tea, coffee, cakes, pastries, nuts and candies, enough to tempt the palate of the greatest epicure, and please the tastes of children. We plain eaters have to pick here and there to get plain food. That dish of hominy that is coming on looks tempting—it is as white as rice. "Hog and hominy," they say, "is western fare." I am sure I can thrive on such white "hominy," let alone the "hog." Bell rings for dinner; all seated and served, when, here we go! "tables tipped," fast on a sand bar. Fire all out, and boiler full of sand, we are floating down the river; an anchor is thrown out, "it drags;" one negro says, "if she passes that point yonder, all h—l can't save her." We are trying to be frightened. Another anchor is thrown out; it "holds her."

Six o'clock P. M.—"She is righted," steam on, and we are moving up the river again—50 miles below Kansas City.

APRIL 30TH.—Here we are, at Kansas City, all safely again on terra firma. Hasten to the hotel—find it very much crowded. Go up, up, up, and up stairs to our lodging rooms.

MAY 1ST.—Take a walk out on to the levee—view the city, and see that it takes but a few buildings in this western world to make a city. The houses and shops stand along on the levee, extending back into the hillsides. The narrow street is literally filled with huge merchandise wagons bound for Santa Fe. The power attached to these wagons is seven or eight and sometimes nine pair of long-eared mules, or as many pair of oxen, with a Mexican driver who wields a whip long enough to reach the foremost pair, and who does not hesitate to use it with severity, and a noise too.

Large droves of cattle are driven into town to be sold to emigrants, who, like us, are going into the Territory. Our husbands are all out to-day buying oxen, provisions and cooking utensils for our ox-wagon journey into the Territory.

This is the eleventh anniversary of my wedding-day, and as I review the past pleasant years as they have passed, one after another, until they now number eleven, a shadow comes over me, as I try to look away into the future and ask, "what is my destiny?" But,

> "Heaven from all creatures hides the book of fate,
> All but the page prescrib'd, their present state."

Ah! away with all these shadowings. We shall be very busy this year in making our home comfortable, so that no time can be spared for that dreaded disease, "home-sickness," to take hold of us, and we mean to obey physical laws, thereby securing to ourselves strength of body and vigor of mind.

MAY 2D.—A lovely day. Our husbands are load-ing the ox-wagons. We have hitherto travelled by steam-power, now we are going to try the virtue there is in ox-power—"slow and steady win the race." All ready! Women with bonnets on, and children waiting impatiently.

Women and children walk along up the hill out of this "*Great City*"—wait under a tree—what a beautiful country is spread out before us! Will our Kansas scenery equal this?

Here come the ox-wagons with their white tops; we shall look like a band of Mormons bound for Salt Lake City—" Come, now, Mrs. V., do n't get into that wagon that is drawn by one red ox and one white one! the driver being a small man with a blue frock on—you know you have a seat in Dr. Thorn's wagon."

One mile from the city, and Dr. Thorn has broke his wagon tongue; it must be sent back to Kansas City to be mended. Fires kindled—women cook-ing—supper eaten sitting round on logs, stones, and wagon tongues. This I am sure is a " pic-nic." We expect "pic-nic" now all the time. We are shaded by the horse-chestnut, sweet walnut, and spreading oak; their branches interwoven with the clinging grape vine. Flowers blooming at our feet, and grass-hoppers in profusion hopping in every direction. This is summer time.

MAY 3D.—The women and children, who slept in

their wagons last night, got a good drenching from the heavy shower. It was fortunate for mother, sister, myself, and children, that lodgings were found for us in a house. My husband said not a rain drop found him; he had the whole wagon to himself, besides all of our Indian blankets. Father, it seems, fell back a little and found a place to camp in a tavern, (not a hotel,) where he fell in with the scores of Georgians who loaded a steamer and came up the river the same time that we did. He said he had to be very shrewd indeed not to have them find out that he was a "Free States" man. These Banditts have been sent in here, and will commit all sorts of depredations on the Free State settlers, and no doubt commit many a bloody murder. Have passed Westport, the foothold for Border-Ruffianism. The town looks new, but the hue is dingy. Our drivers used their goads to hurry up the oxen's heavy tread, for we felt somewhat afraid, for we learned the Georgians had centered here. Here, too, came in the Santa Fe and Indian trade—so here may be seen the huge Mexican wagon, stubborn mule, swarthy driver with his goad-like whip, and the red man of the prairie on his fleet Indian pony, laden with dried meat, furs, and buffalo robes. "What! fast in the mud, and with our wagon tongue broke?" "Why, yes, to be sure." So a long time is spent before my husband and Dr. House can put our vehicle in moving order again. Meanwhile, we women folks and children must sit quietly in the wagon to keep out of the rain,—lunch on soda biscuit, look at the deep, black mud in which our wagon is set, and inhale the sweet odor that comes from the blossoms of the crab-apple trees, that are blooming in sheets of whiteness along the roadside.

"All right" again—our company come along up, (for we had gone along in advance,) and think we have been well paid for our smartness. Find lodgings—"turn in"—head aches hard.

MAY 5TH.—For two days have traveled at a slow rate, over muddy roads, fording rivers, which are swollen from the late rain. Our company are all glad to unpack themselves from their emigrant wagons, and take shelter in what would only pass for apologies for houses at the north—cook our own suppers, and accommodate ourselves to a narrow space (not enough to turn over) while the poppies are being shaken o'er our heads. Our Philadelphian Dr.'s wife (Mrs. Thorn) thinks this is hard fare; she is sick to-night. We find our host once to have hailed from New Hampshire, the "Old Granite State." So he and father are having a familiar dish on times of yore. He is the father of half a dozen children, who, with frizzled heads and staring eyes, (the mother having gone to her long home) are gazing upon us as though they did not often see so many persons at a time. This family are very kind to give up their beds and floor to the weary travelers and take themselves to the loft above.

MAY 6TH.—Dined on the prairie, and gathered flowers, while our tired beasts filled themselves with the fresh, green grass. These prairies spread out far and wide, like a green ocean, and they present something of that optical illusion seen in deserts, called "*mirage*, causing distant objects to be seen double, as if reflected in a mirror, so as to appear as if suspended in the air;" in deserts it presents the appearance of water—here it makes the next wood seem nearer. The sun is just setting; this broad carpet of green will soon take on a darker hue. Yonder is a little wood, and just beyond that they say is a house where we can find lodgings for the night.

Have driven 18 miles to-day, "right smart" for the country. So here we are, all huddled into this little house 12 by 16—cook supper over the fire with the help of "*pot hooks and trammels*"—fill the one bed lengthwise and crosswise; the family of the house take to the trundle-bed, while the floor is covered "two or three times one" with men, women and children, rolled in Indian blankets like silk worms in cocoons.

MAY 8TH.—Found ourselves near the ferry of the Big Osage this morning. Our good host of last night, of whom we bought a cow and calf, paying him $25 in gold, said he would see us all safely over the river, and would pilot us through the water that had flowed over the river's bank for some distance in consequence of the late rain; so our "wagon

beds" were raised up with blocks to keep ourselves
and trunks above water. Our wagon was just on
the point of tipping over, women, children, trunks
and provisions, all into more than a yard deep of
muddy water, when our good host rode up by the
side of our wagon to assist us. I gave Willie into
his arms, and so frightened was I, that I jumped
astride behind him on the horse, (waiting for no ceremony,) and rode safely out. Sent him back for the
rest, but the men had righted the wagon, and they
were safe. Are safely over the Big Osage river, and
are hospitably received here at a Mr. Sells.

MAY 9TH.—Have had our washtub filled with little peach and cherry trees to set in our Kansas
orchard. Have been traveling along on the Missouri
border, but now we turn into Kansas Territory. A
broad green sea of prairie is spread out before us,
and in the distance large mounds stretch themselves
along the horizon; some in the form of cones, others
roof shape—not a tree or shrub shade their summits
or sides, but the bright rays of the morning sun illu-
mine their whole surfaces.

Forded "Mine Creek," and dined again on the
prairie. Nine miles to the next wood. Here we
count the miles from wood to wood, not from hotel
to hotel, or tavern to tavern.

A very large drove of cattle passed us this forenoon, bound for California. We come up to them
now—they have stopped to bait—their drivers with

their mules are watching them that they stray not away, for their pasture is bounded by no fence; scattered over these rolling prairies, and quietly feeding, they remind one of the "cattle upon a thousand hills." The appearance is rich—it must be an oriental picture.

Our slow coaches have come 18 miles to-day—women and children are all tired, tired, tired—find comfortable lodgings, and here on this bed canopied with white curtains, I will lay my aching head—don't want any supper.

MAY 11TH.—"Made" but a few miles yesterday. Forded the Little Osage; the last river, they say, we have to ford; and it was a very difficult one too, on account of such steep banks and muddy bottom. Our "noble lords" complained of the great weight of the wagons. They were obliged to attach all the oxen to one wagon, draw that through and up the steep bank, then take another, and so on until all were through and up the bank.

That *our* wagon is heavily loaded, have only to to make a minute of what we have stowed away in it—eight trunks, one valise, three carpet bags, a box of soda crackers, 200 lbs. flour, 100 lbs. corn meal, a few lbs. of sugar, rice, dried apple, one washtub of little trees, utensils for cooking, and two provision boxes—say nothing of mother, a good fat sister, self, and two children, who ride through the rivers.

At nightfall came to a log-cabin at the edge of a

wood, and inquired of the "Lord of the Castle" if some of the women and children could take shelter under his roof for the night; the masculine number and whichever of the women that chose, couching in the wagons and under them. He said we could. His lady, who was away, presently came, with bare feet, and a white sack twisted up and thrown over her shoulder, with a few quarts of corn meal in the end that hung down her back. I said to myself— "Is that what I have got to come to?" She seemed pleased to have company—allowed us the first chance of the broad, Dutch-backed fireplace with its earthy hearth, and without *pot-hooks or trammels*, to make ready our simple evening repast.

A bed was made for us on the floor; she bade us put our shoes and stockings under our heads, or the rats would carry them off. And we thought before morning that they would take us bodily, not minding the small articles, such as shoes and stockings, there came such "a power" of the "critters," as these southern people say.

A large, black wild turkey lay with its head stretched over a log this morning, which our host had just shot. He said, "There's a right smart chance for game here." His better-half thought we had "mighty fine children" and a "power of folks."

Are now crossing the 20 mile prairie, no roads— keep pilots ahead to pilot us around ravines and keep us out of gulches, (as the deep places are called.) Think Mrs. Voorhees will get walking enough crossing this prairie. She is quite a pedestrian surely, for she has walked every bit of the way in, so far, from Kansas City, almost 100 miles.

Arrive at Elm Creek—no house to lodge in to-night—camp-fire kindled—supper cooked, and partaken of with a keen relish, sitting in family groups around the "great big" fire. Some will sleep in wagons, others under the canopy of the blue vault of Heaven. The young men have built some shady little bowers of the green boughs; they are looking very cosily under them, wrapped in their white Indian blankets. It was very fortunate that we took along the bale of blankets from Kansas City, belonging to the company. My husband paid $20 freightage on them, but we are getting that much good from them while emigrating.

We ladies, or rather "emigrant women," are having a chat around the camp-fire—the bright stars are looking down upon us—we wonder if we shall be neighbors to each other in the great "Octagon City." The Dr.'s wife says, a lady in Philadelphia has promised to send her embroidery. I am thinking we shall have little call for embroidery for the next three years.

MAY 12TH.—Full of hope, as we leave the smoking embers of our camp-fire this morning. Expect to-night to arrive at our new home.

It begins to rain, rain, rain, like a shower; we move slowly on, from high prairie, around the deep ravine—are in sight of the timber that skirts the Neosho river. Have sent three men on in advance to announce our coming; are looking for our Secretary, (Henry S. Clubb) with an escort to welcome us into the embryo city. If the booming of cannon is not heard at our approach, shall expect a salute from the firing of Sharp's rifles, certainly.

No escort is seen! no salute is heard! We move slowly and drippingly into town just at nightfall—feeling not a little nonplused on learning that our worthy, or unworthy Secretary was out walking in the rain with his *dear* wife. We leave our wagons and make our way to the large camp-fire. It is surrounded by men and women cooking their suppers—while others are busy close by, grinding their hominy in hand mills.

Look about, and see the grounds all around the camp-fire are covered with tents, in which the families are staying. Not a house is to be seen. In the large tent here, is a cook stove—they have supper prepared for us; it consists of hominy, not soft Johnny-cake, (or corn bread, as it is called here,) stewed apple, and tea. We eat what is set before us, "asking no questions for conscience' sake."

The ladies tell us they are sorry to see us come to this place; which plainly shows that all is not right. Are too weary to question, but with hope depressed go to our lodgings, which we find around in the tents, and in our wagons.

CHAPTER III.

"On each condition disappointments wait,
    Enter the hut, and force the guarded gate."

ALSO—"Disappointment lurks in many a prize."

MAY 13TH.—Can any one imagine our disappointment this morning, on learning from this and that member, that no mills have been built; that the directors, after receiving our money to build mills, have not fulfilled the trust reposed in them, and that in consequence, some families have already left the settlement.

Now *we all have come!* have brought our fathers, our mothers, and our little ones, and find no shelter sufficient to shield them from the furious prairie winds, and the terrific storms of the climate!

For a moment let me contrast the two pictures—the one we had made provision for, and had reason to believe would be presented to us, with the one that meets our eyes:

Expected a saw-mill would be in operation, a grist-mill building, and a temporary boarding-house erected to receive families as they should come into the settlement, until their own houses could be built.

Wherever there are mills in this south-western world, there surely is to be a town. And how much of life, active life, would resound through a new settlement, from the noisy saw-mill, the filing of the saw, and the handing out of new, clean, white boards. How soon could comfortable houses be built; and hope and animation light up every father's and mother's face. As it is, we find the families, some living in tents of cloth, some of cloth and green bark just peeled from the trees, and some wholly of green bark, stuck up on the damp ground, without floors or fires. Only two stoves in the company. These intelligent, but too confiding, families have come from the North, East, South and West, to this *farther* West, to make pleasant homes; and now are determined to turn right about, start again on a journey—some know not where! Others have invested their all in the company. Now come lost means and blighted hopes.

We see that the city grounds, which have been surveyed, (and a log cabin built in the centre, where is to stand the large "central octagon building,") are one mile from here. It seems the company did not pitch their tents there, on account of its being so wet, so chose this higher prairie until after the spring rains should be over. . Two or three families of us, and a few single men, take to our wagons again, drive over the roadless prairie, and around the head of a creek, to become the first residents in the "Neosho, or Octagon City." Find the city, as we had seen, to contain only one log cabin, 16 by 16, mudded between the logs on the inside, instead of on the outside; neither door nor window; the roof covered with "shakes," (western shingles,) split out of oak I should think, 3 1-2 feet in length, and about as wide as a sheet of fools cap paper.

The men have set themselves at work now to improve this dwelling. Some are laying a floor, or rather paving one, by drawing fresh dirt, spreading it all over the ground, then laying flat stones of irregular shape on to it, leaving them bound on all sides by the rich prairie soil. Others are laying a floor to the loft above, of "shakes," doubled and trebled, they being just long enough to lap from beam to beam, which from their slivery sides and warping propensity, methinks, will present no very smooth surface to lie upon, when nothing, hardly, save one Indian blanket is to intervene between us and them.

My husband is making a ladder, by way of easy ascent to our dormitory. The bed-ticks, comfortables, few sheets and pillows, that we took the precaution to put in our trunks, I think will be duly appreciated.

MAY 14TH.—Some improvements are being made in the "centre octagon" to-day. My husband has put up some shelves on one side, by boring holes into the logs, putting in long and strong wooden pins, and laying on some of the "shakes" for shelves. Have arranged on them our five tin plates, two tin cups, one tin tumbler, the nine tea-plates I brought in my trunk, one cream cup, knives, forks, spoons, and the covered tin pail that holds our milk. Underneath stand our provision pails and cooking utensils. Mrs. V. has a shelf appropriated to her use. A pole bedstead is made, corded with strips of bark, and a tick filled with dry prairie grass we have gathered here and there; so a bed is made up and placed in one corner on the bare stone floor, to be occupied by father and mother. Placed some of the trunks in another corner for a lounge for sister L., for she dare not risk her fat sides up the ladder, on to our "shaky" floor. The bags of flour, meal, salt, etc., are set in the third corner, while along towards the shelves stands the cracker bag, and on its lowered contents have put our small quantity of groceries— tea, sugar, rice, and baking powder. The fourth and south-eastern corner is where we go out doors, stepping over a threshhold about a foot high. Keep the wash-tub sitting handily by, for with it turned bottom side up, two provision pails, and one end-board of the wagon, we make a table; then gathering around our both circular and parallelogramic table, some on trunks, others on their elbows, partake of our simple meal; each one trying all the time to appear cheerful—trying to make the best of present condition, while a heavy weight is resting upon each one's heart. Have found a piece of a little round log, just long enough for my children to sit on. On it they sit and eat their food from their plates and out of their tin cups. They say "this is a funny way to eat." Our small trunks are set back and used for chairs.

MAY 15TH.—A cold, drizzling rain. The prairie winds come whizzing in. Have hung up an Indian blanket at the door, but by putting trunks and even stones on to the end that drags, can hardly make it answer the purpose of a door. It is dark, gloomy, cheerless, uncomfortable and cold inside.

Have a fire out of doors to cook by ; two crotches driven into the ground, with a round pole laid thereon, on which to hang our kettles and camp pails, stones laid up at the ends and back to make it as much as it can be in the form of a fireplace, so as to keep our fire, ashes and all, from blowing high and dry, when these fierce prairie winds blow. It is not very agreeable work, cooking out of doors in this windy, rainy weather, or when the scorching sun shines.

The bottoms of our dresses are burnt full of holes now, and they will soon be burnt off. If we stay here we must needs don the Bloomer costume. Our bill of fare is limited ; we do not ask, "what shall we have good for dinner ?" or "what delicacy for tea ?" something to please the palate, for it is the same simple dishes, right over and over again : hominy, johnny cake, Graham pudding, *some* white bread,

4

now and then stewed apple, a little rice, and tea occasionally for the old people.

Our excellent cow, that came so gently into the Territory, tied to the back end of our wagon, supplies us and her calf with fresh, rich milk; no place to set it however, and nothing to set it in, does away with the work of churning. Pies, cakes, butter, etc., would be superfluous articles in these "diggins."

Father has got a broom stick, and is peeling a broom; he says, "I intend you shall keep this stone floor swept up clean."

MAY 16TH.—Still rainy, damp and cold. My husband has brought in the two side-boards that fill the vacancy between between the "wagon bed" and the white cover, has laid them side by side in the loft above, and says, "Miriam, you may make your bed on the smooth surface of these two boards." I say to him, "No; as you have to work hard, you shall have the boards, and with one pillow and your blanket, you will have an even bed, though it is hard. I will take the other pillow, the comfortable and blankets, and with the children will couch close by, endeavoring to suit myself to the warpings, rough edges and lappings, of our 'shaky' floor." A few feet from me and the children, Mr. and Mrs. V. have their quilt and blanket spread; while a foot or two from their heads can be seen Dr. House and Mr. Sober, mummies in their Indian blankets. So every part of the "centre octagon" is appropriated. Hear that others are coming from the tents to quarter here—and if they do, why then, I suppose, we must "hitch" along and make room for them.

My husband has had a talk with our Secretary, who says, "I expect a saw-mill on from St. Louis, and the fourth company soon."

We feel a little more hopeful, and conclude that, seeing we have come so heavily laden with our friends, we had better stay in this country, and take our fortune as it may come.

MAY 17TH.—The greater number of the company that came in with us, and others that were here, left this morning for Kansas City; and from there they know not where they will go! They feel so much disappointed, they care not to go home again, and indeed some have not the means. It is saddening to think about.

MAY 18TH.—Some of the settlers from up the siver called in to see us to-day, it being Sunday, and *their day* to make calls. Among them was one *Henly*, a smooth-tongued, oily-mouthed fellow, that caused a chill to pass over me to look at; the reason my intuition does not define. I asked them if they were Border Ruffians, after which my husband chided me, said I must be careful what I said to strangers.

Have tried to quiet my mind, to read some, but surrounded by so many discomforts and anxieties, I refuse "to be comforted."

MAY 19TH.—Mrs. V., sister L. and self, have been
to the creek and done up our last month's washing.
Had the inconveniences of hard water, a scanty supply of soap, and only a one-pail full camp-pail to
boil in. Expected our Secretary, who was to purchase necessary articles for the settlers, would not
neglect to have a supply of one of the most necessary articles, *soap*. Starching and ironing will be
dispensed with, for the want of what we have been
in the habit of calling *indispensable, flat-irons*. A
rub through the hand is all my own and the children's clothes can have, and the same will be done
to their papa's linen, though that is to be exchanged
now for the striped blue wear.

MAY 20TH.—Have been busy all day in my kitch-
en, whose dimensions are by no means confining. It
is roofed by the blue dome of heaven, the partition
wall on the south, is the timber that fringes the Neosho; on the north, east, and west, the smooth green
prairie, gently swelling, declining, then swelling
higher again, until in the distance it is joined with
the roofing of blue. Not a cloud has pictured its
vault; but yonder "king of day" has sent down his
rays with scorching effect. Have raised salt yeast
by keeping it covered tightly in a kettle of warm
water, to exclude the ashes and flying dirt—raised
the bread and baked in a Dutch oven. The oven is
small, could only bake one loaf at a time. The
wind has blown so hard, that I was obliged to lay

up stones all around the oven to keep the coals under it; made a fire on the top of chips, laying stones on to the chips, to keep them confined so as to serve my use. Have really labored hard all day, and have baked only two small loaves of bread, while, in a family of seven, like ours, one can be dispatched at each meal.

MAY 22D.—Members of the company, who have concluded to remain in the Territory, think it time now to do what they can, under present disappointments, for the comfort of their families, and also for their future welfare. Some are building their cabins on their city lots, in their respective portions of the octagon; others, independent of the company, have become "squatter sovereigns," and will build their cabins on their claims.

Each claimant can claim and hold, by the preemption right, 240 acres of land—160 timber, and 80 prairie. My husband, his father, and sister L. are each claimants; they have accordingly located their claims side by side, making 720 acres of land belonging to our family. It is two miles east from the "centre octagon," and joining the Osage Indian lands. My husband says, the timber on our claim is fine; there are different kinds of walnut and oak, (some black walnuts 4 feet through,) and that for several rods on the river is the prettiest bed of pebbles he ever saw, nice for walks. We intend, some time, to have walks made of them.

The Stewarts have located their claims two miles west from here; are building their cabin on a high prairie swell, where nature has planted the walnut and oak just sparsely enough for both beauty and shade.   Just back, and south of the cabin, is a ledge of shelving rocks, where many berry bushes have taken root in the vegetable mould in their crevices, and are clinging for support to their craggy sides. Grape vines clamber over rock, shrub and tree. There is a natural cut through the ledge, and an Indian trail leading down to a quiet little lake, sleeping in among the tall grass, whose waters abound in fish and clams.   The whole view is beautifully picturesque.

Mr. Adams has made a cabin of "shakes" on his city lot, one-fourth of a mile north from the "centre."

Mr. Herriman, a little shed-like cabin of logs and bark, one-half mile, a little west of north.

The Broadbents have pitched their tent on their city lot, one mile north.

H. S. Clubb's dwelling is a cabin made of an old Indian wigwam and tenting, one mile south-east, on his city lot.

Father Cosgrove resides in a cabin of "shakes," one-half mile south-east, on his city lot, near the river.

The Ohio men have the large tent; it is pitched on Mr. Wheeler's lot, one-half mile north-west, just across the creek that rises from a spring near the Broadbents, and empties into the Neosho.

Mr. Hubbs has a cabin of "shakes" and cloth, one mile south-west, near the river.

Mr. Voorhees will plant his corn on his city lot, but for the present will live here in the "centre octagon," with us.

The young men, and men without their families, board around in the cabins with the families. So we are all uncomfortably situated, for the want of proper building materials.

CHAPTER IV.

Speed the ONE PLOUGH, boys, plant the bright corn;
Summer's upon us—the work should be done,
That Autumn may crown with bright yellow ears—
Hope to enliven—and quiet our fears.

MAY 24TH.—A very busy time now, with each
man, only one plough in the company, (except Mr.
Stewart's) and every man wants to use that at the
same time. My husband has ploughed nights; some
of these lovely moonlit nights. It is time that our
corn and seeds were planted, though they say that
corn will ripen in this climate, planted in July.

Have been over to see Mrs. Herriman, poor sick
woman! She is suffering severely with the inflam-
matory rheumatism; sometimes she seems to be in
perfect anguish—could not móve her hands at all
to-day. Cannot take any care of her little one, now
nearly two months old. It was presented to her
while on her journey into the Territory—delaying
the company only two days. She was very smart
indeed, but so many exposures have brought this
dreadful disease upon her. Her cabin is very uncom-

fortable, with a shed roof, which covers it but a little more than half way over with bark, a fire in one corner against the green logs, a ground floor, and no door. She cannot bear to hear a word about staying in this country. I picked a lovely bouquet of prairie flowers and carried to her, but she could not take them into her hands; so I put them into a phial of water and hung them to one of the bark covered logs over head, so that she could look at them.

MAY 25TH.—This is a most lovely day. Hope is lightening up the hearts of the settlers. The spring rains are giving way to bright and lovely weather, and summer-time is coming with its beautiful array of lovely, bright-eyed flowers.

The climate of this Eastern Kansas is said to resemble that of Virginia, only more balmy. The winter lasts from Christmas until the last of January or the first of February—then trees can be set, and all kinds of planting done, from that time until July. Some seeds yield two crops a year.

This part of Kansas " is attended with rains from the beginning of March until June. The streams are swollen; and wagon routes become miry, but not like those of Indiana and Illinois; and it is not probable that corduroy or plank roads will need be constructed." "The vegetation is exuberant."

The summer is long; high noon is fanned by the south wind from the Cordilleras, keeping off the intense heat, which otherwise would be almost unbearable. Dewy, cool nights. No long rains through the summer or autumn; showers come up quickly with tremendous and deafening thunder—one glare of lightning, and rain in torrents—as quickly clear away, leaving the moistened earth to heave with luxuriance.

"Autumn brings the calm beauty of the Indian Summer of New England and the Middle States," "is rather dry—creeks stand in pools." "But the crops are harvested, so matured as not to be injured by the drouth." There is one sunlit season, from October until December, when all the crickets and katy-dids are finishing up through the live-long nights, their last autumnal songs.

Max. Greene further says of this country:—

"Throughout the Osage country, there are scenes of romantic loveliness; and some even bordering on the picturesque. In tranquil summer-time, it has the plain, yet dreamy beauty of the Flemish landscape. Over all, a Sabbath serenity is diffused; and grassy knoll and leafy wood are embathed in a soft and subdued lustre, which is indescribably soothing and inspires holiest impulses. Remembrances come to me now of one full August of soul-felt enjoyment, because it was a life so novel and so free, every evening of which my blanket was spread upon one or the other of its tufted hill-tops. Then goldenly the sun would go down, and crimson bannerets of clouds would follow in his royal wake. The tall grass

would wave beneath the zephyr, stealing up like a
pet bird of the stillest wing from the twilight reaches
of the dell beneath. The swarthy figure of some
solitary Indian horseman would flit near and disap-
pear by a path leading into the hollow of a stream."

In my rambles on the bottom lands and on the
banks of the Neosho, have seen the large black walnut, the white or shag-bark, the hickory, different
kinds of oak, ash, willow, and numberless small trees
that I could not name—then the large, spreading
sycamore with its white trunk, extended spectral
limbs and broad green leaves. The grape-vine clam-
bers from tree to tree, weaving its tendrils through
all their branches, making one complete arbor all in
among the forest trees. While lower down, all the
shrubs are interlaced with the hop vine, climbing
roses, and many geranium-like vines. Under foot
were blooming whole garden-like beds of flowers—
all strangers to me, aside from the mandrake or May
apple, adder's tongue, violets, and splendid verbenas.
On the banks of the Neosho grow plum trees and
gooseberry bushes; along the gulches, ravines and
creeks, grow black raspberries and running black-
berries, clasping whatever grows near them. Find
the Neosho to be as dark and muddy a stream as
the Missouri; high banks, which are overflown in
the spring, the water carrying off all the harvest of
nuts of the previous fall from the bottom lands, down
to the Arkansas river, and from thence onward to
the Mississippi. It is not serviceable for mill pur-

poses, as has been represented. The water is so low
in summer-time that one can walk over it on the
stones. We find plenty of water now; springs come
bubbling out from every dell, and brooklets from
every gulch. I have picked up many petrified pieces
of limbs of trees, in the spring where I go for water,
also other fossils.

Have not allowed the children to stir from the
cabin alone, for fear of the snakes; but a few minutes ago gave them permission to go a few rods to
pick some roses. Mema soon came running in, saying: "O! papa, I see a little snake out here." Her
papa went out, and just where they were picking
roses lay a great gray rattlesnake. He killed the
snake and threw it away in the grass. I asked him
why he did not take out the rattles. He said, "I
cannot do such a piece of dirty work."

Notwithstanding the snakes,

"If thou would'st find a favored land,
    By Nature's chosen bounties blest—
A fertile soil, a climate bland—
    Come seek the regions of the West.

"Here is the farmer's paradise;
    Rich harvests come with little care,
While spreading rivers brimming rise
    And to their marts these products bear."

MAY 26TH.—Have been washing to-day, and dried
our clothes right out in the burning hot sun. We
dare not leave them out in the dewy nights, for fear

of the Indians, who come thieving round—slying about—taking everything they can lay their hands on ; pieces of rope, cord, strings, twine, matches, and bits of paper, which are all valuable to us now, on account of their scarcity. They are soon going two or three hundred miles west on their buffalo hunt, where they go twice or thrice a year, staying three months at a time. Game is getting scarce in this region, and is confined to deer, wild turkeys, prairie hens, and small game. Plenty of large birds abound in the waters of the Neosho.

It is rumored here that these Osage Indians are at war with one of the savage tribes of the western mountains, and if they gain the victory, they will take their hunting grounds, and leave this part of the territory. If I am to live here, I can't but secretly hope it may be so.

These Indians are said to be friendly, but I cannot look at their painted visages without a shudder ; and when they come around our cabin, I sit down and take Willie on my lap, and have Mema stand by my side, with my arm around her, for fear they may steal my children from me. They point to my boy and make signs that he is pretty. "Chintu-chinka," they call boy, and "che-me chinka," girl.

This is a new country to the white man ; every scene affirms it, yet for ages unknown these green expansive prairie meadows have been traversed by the red man. Here he has built his wigwam—here hunted the wild game, not more wild than himself

—here sounded the war-whoop—here smoked the calumet of peace—and here worshipped the "Great I Am," in the simple way He could be presented to his savage wild nature. He leaves no traces of civilization—all his prints are Indian—wild—his hard trodden roads of one foot in width cross and and re-cross this country in every possible direction. It seems almost useless to try to inject civilization into his veins, otherwise than by amalgamation with with the Anglo-Saxon race, which is now being done —fading out the red of the race. There are thousands of half-breeds, now living in cabins, cultivating the soil, and keeping herds of cattle.

" The whole Indian population of Kansas, at the present time, is probably twenty-five thousand, scattered over a territory of eighty-one millions of acres." Four thousand Osages just across the Neosho from us, living in their city of wigwams. They take life easy, depending upon their hunting tours and their annuities from the government, for support.

Some of these Indians dress, others dress but little except a breech cloth, moccasins, deer-skin leggins, to keep off the snakes, and their blankets. They come into our cabin, and sit down; while sitting, their blankets slide from their shoulders, revealing their large, dark, brown, and nearly nude forms, to the shudder of the unaccustomed beholder.

They are tall, well-formed, and straight as an arrow. They shave their hair, leaving only a lock on the top of the head; they then rub paint all in their growing hair, and paint their faces, arms and breasts. They are very fond of ornaments; it seems as though their necks must groan under the weight of fancy beads. The rim of their ears is slit clear around, and filled with jewels of brass and tin, some of gold, and some fill the slitted rim with flowers and eagle feathers. I have seen some Indians wear little bells, strung on a strip of deer skin, and fastened around their legs just below the knee, making a noise for them every time they stirred. The squaws wear their long black hair hanging down their backs. They dress in calico loose-gowns and "brief" skirts; ornament with beads and jewels, but not so heavily as the Indians.

MAY 28TH.—Took my children into our white-toped wagon, and went with my husband two miles, to his claim, to plant corn. A bright and lovely day came in with the rising sun, not a cloud in the heavens above, and one carpet of green spread far and wide below, ornamented with thousands of new-blown flowers, scenting the air with a mixture of their rich perfumes. Not a stump, fence, stone or log, to mar the beautiful picture. "Ah!" I exclaimed, "here is too much beauty to look upon at once, for one whose heart wears the gloom of disappointment and the forebodings of fear." We sat in the wagon, while my hopeful husband planted corn

and garden seeds. After the ploughing, the planting is done by just cutting through the sod with an
axe, and dropping in the seeds—no hoeing the first
year; nothing more is to be done until the full yellow
ears are gathered in the autumn time.

I gathered flowers for the children, listened to
their soothing prattle, and thought as I have often
thought, "how beautiful would this natural Eden
look, if parted off with fences into farms, dotted over
with cities, villages and farm-houses; the tall church
spires reaching up into the clear blue sky, the round
domes reflecting the bright sunshine, and the smoke
seen in the distance, of the noisy locomotives chasing
each other over these flowery meadows, bringing
welcome faces and speedy news from home-land, and
trade from north, east, south and west. I am sorry
to breathe out, as I do sometimes, (for it damps the
others' ardor,) that my hope is a star that has set.

After we had eaten our dinner in the wagon, we
went and selected a site for our log cabin, a little
way from the clear, stony-bottomed creek that flows
through our claim. The land lies a little inclining
south towards the river, and the clear waters of the
little creek will flow quietly along by our cabin
door. The spider-wort blooms in acres of blue, all
around; and the sensitive plant, with its slightly
briery running stalk, covered all over with flowers
of pink balls dotted with yellow, and its tiny leaves
that shrink from the least touch, sends out its scent

of otto of roses to meet your olfactories, some rods before you reach it.

My husband says we shall have an elegant building spot, that he will build a neat little log cabin, and have the cellar so as to open into it from one side: that on the outside it will be a mound, which we can ornament with vines and flowers; that he will get the large flat stones from the creek, that will cleave apart, for walks to the creek and around our cabin; and that he thinks, when we come to get our goods, have our carpets to spread on our rough floors, our nice little stove to cook by, our bedsteads, dishes, and all the necessaries and comforts our boxes contain, together with our books, that we shall be comfortably situated—shall be "squatter sovereigns" indeed. I do not like to hear that voice which whispers, "this never will be;" but still it will whisper.

MAY 30TH.—Am wearing the Bloomer dresses now; find they are well suited to a wild life like mine. Can bound over the prairies like an antelope, and am not in so much danger of setting my clothes on fire, while cooking when these prairie winds blow. Have had Mrs. Herriman's baby here for a few days, she is so very sick. Mr. H. wanted to plant his corn and garden seeds; he could leave his sick wife with the little two-year-old boy, but could not leave the little one to cry when its mother could not stir to take care of it. Mrs. V. has taken most of the care of it while here.

5

Have been over to see Mrs. H. ; she is some better. Picked another bouquet of very rich flowers on my way, and placed them for her to look at; there were Japan lilies, large beautiful snake's-head, larkspurs of many colors, and much larger than those we cultivate at home; prairie roses of every shade and variegation, golden coreopsis, sweet William, and a variety of others that were strangers to me. Wild peas and beans are scattered broadcast over these green fields; their blossoms are very pretty; they are eaten by the Indians; are said to make good coffee, and when green they are sometimes pickled. Beds and beds of onions are growing here and there, with the little onions all clustered in on the top, not larger than kernels of wheat.

I will take time now to describe a novel picture that met my gaze a few evenings ago, as my husband and self were returning from Mr. Stewart's. Just as we neared the creek, on the other side, a little way up, saw a smoke and a few Indians. Our curiosity soon led us to the spot. One squaw was very busy cooking their supper. She had two stakes driven into the ground, meeting at the top, and a chain suspended between them, on which hung a brass kettle filled with dried apples, stewing. Down before the fire, she was frying cakes in buffalo grease. Her dough was wet up in a tin pan, and she was making them out round on the bottom of an iron dish, cutting them across grid-iron fashion. She had already a stack one foot in height; they looked

brown and inviting. On each side of her stood her
two little twin Indian boys; when they saw me,
they cried and cried, and hid their black heads under their mother's loose-gown. I spoke to them, but
they only cried the harder, and cuddled up the closer
to their mother, making it difficult for her to tend
the frying cakes. So I told them I would not talk
to them or hurt them. Of course they understood
my language. Close by lay an old Indian on a
blanket, groaning with severe pain in one shoulder.
Young squaw was cupping his shoulder in their savage
age way, by first hacking it with one of their large
Indian knives, then placing the large end of a buffalo horn over it, and exhausting the air with her
mouth through "the little end of the horn," spitting
the blood from her mouth which she had drawn from
the wounds.

We heard, afterward, that the old Indian's shoulder was out of joint, and that he sent up the river
for a white doctor, who set it, and exacted an Indian pony, worth fifty or sixty dollars, which he got.
White men triumph over the "big trades" they
make with the red men of the plains; a little coffee,
sugar, and whiskey, will go a great way in paying
them off. "Is it right?" I ask. Three dollars for
a buffalo robe, worth twelve at home.

JUNE 1ST.—Church at Mr. Clubb's. Mr. Clubb
read a sermon. That will be our present place of
worship. Suppose sometime, when our settlement

gets flourishing enough, our tall church spire will
stretch heavenward, and we shall be called to worship by

> " The sound of the church-going bell
>   These valleys and rocks never heard ;
>   Ne'er sigh'd at the sound of a knell,
>   Or smiled when a Sabbath appeared."

We find the most of our company to profess the
Presbyterian faith.

I am thankful that wherever our lot may be cast,
we can worship the *Upholder of the Universe* in
temples not made with hands.   This quiet Sabbath
eve is a fit time for retrospection—to think of all the
pleasant surroundings and privileges we were wont
to share, away in our Northern homes.

> " Oh, had I the wings of a dove,
>   How soon would I taste you again ! "

JUNE 3D. — Many an acre of prairie is now
ploughed, and planted with corn ; looks quite like
farming, and our corn will be our hope for next winter's provision.   The grass is getting high, and to
walk through it on a dewy morning one gets as wet
as though they had forded a river.   The cattle fill
themselves with the fresh feed to a monstrous size.
They mow down the spider-wort with its blue flowers and juicy stalks, with great eagerness—the juice
fairly dripping from each corner of their mouths.
One of our oxen was so bloated this morning, we
thought he would die ; is better now.

A most terrific thunder-storm came up last night; the thunder tumbled from the sky, crash upon crash, as though all was being rolled together like a scroll; the fiery chains of lightning streaked the heavens from zenith to horizon. The rain came in torrents, and the wind blew almost tornadoes. Our cabin, seemingly, was but little security against its wildness. When we heard the storm approaching, we dressed ourselves, wrapping Indian blankets about us, and made ready to protect our children from the rain, that was then dripping through the roof. We put all our bedding around them, and all we could see to get by the glare of the lightning, (could not keep a candle lit,) spread our umbrellas, (five in number,) placed about, and held over them. We all got wet, and were obliged to lie in our wet beds till morning. This morning all was calm; the bright sun ascended up into a cloudless sky, as majestically as though there had been no war in the elements through the night. But the rain had dissolved our mud chinking, and the wind had strewed it all over and in our beds, on our clothes, over our dishes, and into every corner of the house. Have had all our sheets to wash, beds and blankets to dry in the sun and rub up, our log walls to sweep down, our shelves and dishes to clean, and our *own selves* to brush up. " Such is prairie life," so they say.

JUNE 5TH.—Our young and very much respected Mr. Sober, has left the settlement, and gone back to

his home in Michigan.   There are too few prospects
here for him.   Mr. Voorhees comes in, sits down on
the lowest round of the ladder, holds his head down,
and looks sad.   I am sure the star of hope is not
very high here for him, notwithstanding all the natural resources of this beautiful country for making
it a favored land.   Disappointment has darkened
every brow, however hard they may have striven to
rise above it.   We are 100 miles from a grist-mill;
and 50 from a post office.   Mr. Clubb has petitioned
to have the mail come here.

The Indians have gone away now on their hunt;
it seems quiet and good to have our fear removed
for a time.   The people say we have had our hard-
est time here, but it does not seem so to me.   I oft-
en ask myself, "Why do I have so many presentiments of coming sorrow?"   The dark storm-clouds,
(to my mind's eye,) are gathering in our horizon,
and even now they flap their cold, bat-like wings
about my head, causing my heart to tremble with
fear.   I am so impressed some nights with this feeling, that I sit up in bed for hours, and fairly cringe
from some unknown terror.   I tell my husband,
"We are a doomed ship; unless we go away, some
great calamity will come upon us; and it is on me
that the storm will burst with all its dark fury."
Sometimes a voice speaks to me in thunder tones,
saying, "Rise, rise! flee to the mountains,—tarry
not in all the plain.   Haste away!   Destruction 's
before thee, and sorrow behind;" and, "you never

will be a happy family again." I call Willie to me, put my hand on his head, and weep and weep, and say, "O, Willie! Willie! Willie!" My husband says, "Miriam, don't feel so; I am afraid you will go crazy. I think it is your imaginings, caused by our disappointments and discomforts." I answer, "I hope it is, but I don't know why I should be so overpowered with such feelings; they come to me without being invited, and I cannot help giving them expression sometimes."

JUNE 7TH.—My husband is up at his claim planting corn. Hopeful man! Whatever of calamity may be pent up in the black clouds for us, may Heaven grant that our lives may be spared! I can bear all pecuniary losses,—go hungry, cold, barefoot, and sleep on the rough and uneven floor,—but spare me my beloved husband and my darling children.

The *one plough* is broken. Father started off this morning to go twenty-five miles, down to the Catholic Mission, where is the nearest blacksmith, to get it mended. Mrs. Herriman and her two children are here; she is better. They intend leaving the Territory in two or three days. I am cooking some victuals for them to take on their solitary journey over the prairies. We are as much shut out from the world here as though we were on some lonely island in the ocean; and it requires almost as much skill to navigate these green seas of grass, with prairie, gulch and dell, as it does the distant blue seas of water, with their islands and rock-bound coasts.

I have cooked so much out in the hot sun and smoke, that I hardly know who I am, and when I look in the little looking-glass I ask, "Can this be me?" Put a blanket over my head, and I would pass well for an Osage squaw. My hands are the color of a smoked ham, and get so burnt that the skin peels off one after another. I should feel happy if we were going along with Mr. Herriman, as he wants us to.

JUNE 9TH.—Mr. Herriman started off this morning with his ox-wagon, sick wife, and two little children. It will be necessary for him to be navigator, driver, nurse to his sick wife, and carer for the little ones. They intend to journey thus to some northern town in Illinois. But they have, to cheer them on, the hope that they are traveling world-ward, and every mile will take them nearer to civilization and a better home. They have given their little puppy, "Sambo dog," to Willie. He is very much pleased with it, but don't like to have it bite his apron. He says, "See, mamma, Sambo bites Willie's apron!" This little chestnut-colored dog with his large drooping ears and profuse "bow-wow" when anybody is coming, will be a pet dog, and a great deal of company for the children.

Father has returned with the mended plough—has had quite an interesting time going to and from the

blacksmith's shop, a journey of fifty miles. Took
dinner to-day at the house of Mr. Godfrey, the Indian Agent, feasted on green corn, beans, pease, and
cucumbers. A nice fresh dinner surely! Mr. Godfrey is married to one of the Osage squaws. She
has mounted her pony, left her white husband to attend to business, and gone with her tribe on the
buffalo hunt. Mrs. Godfrey has a Rocky Mountain
Indian maid, that was taken captive by the Osages
for her waiting maid. Without doubt Mrs. G. will
enjoy the wild chase far beyond any sips of civilization.

JUNE 10TH.—Mr. Clubb has returned from Fort
Scott, and the goods, groceries, seeds, and some provisions belonging to the company, have arrived.
They were bought with the company's money, still
we are charged a very high price for them. Potatoes four dollars per bushel; can't afford to have
even one meal of them—have cooked one for mother;
they must, all that we have, be planted. Flour is
dealt out to us in rations. Have just been to Mr.
Clubb's with my small white bag; came home with
a few pounds in one end strung over my shoulder.
I must have resembled the Missourian woman, with
her bag of corn meal, (for I felt as she looked) when
I said, "shall I ever come to this?"

On my way home called on "father" Cosgrove;
he was planting pea-nuts. He is expecting to dig
them out of the ground by the bushel in autumn.

I hear that Mrs. Clubb felt greatly annoyed while her husband was away, by an intruder at her feet in the night time; in the morning found that a large rattlesnake had been occupying the bed with herself. They are fond of a comfortable place to coil up in.

JUNE 12TH.—Yesterday father gave us an invitation to take a ride out into this roadless country. Soon Mrs. V., sister L., myself and children were in our covered wagon, and the oxen bore us slowly over the prairie, nipping and crushing the flowers as they went. The first of June is the time for flowers—the broad, wild parterre is now glowing with thousands of them, from the richest hue to the most delicate tint. We passed broad beds of portulacca blooming in its richness in the bright sunshine, while near its large beds of bright sunny flowers, the prickly pear was growing in luxuriant clumps, ornamented with large yellow flowers dotted with black, which on touching would give sharp intimations of their nature.

When five miles away out on the high prairies, we came to the ruins of a city of Indian wigwams, long since untenanted. We saw no obelisks crumbling away—no sculptured marble broken—no granite walls tumbling down—no relict of dome, turret, or spire—but the rude dilapidation pictured the undeveloped mechanism of the red man, his poverty of tools, and want of knowledge to use them. Their wigwams, I should think, were first commenced by driving into the ground "punchuns," (their Indian boards split out of logs, about five feet in length and as wide as the log is thick,) about one foot, making a close upright fence, extending rods in length, and about one in width. Then poles were fastened and bent from each side, lapping past a large pole in the middle over head, which made the ridge pole. This pole frame was covered with mats made of the cat-tail flag, or buffalo skins. These long, rough ter-races were then divided off into tenements. Streets of two or three rods in width separated these many terarces. There were buffalo horns in profusion, buffalo skins and mats in piles, once the covering of the wigwams. There were tin pans, plates, tin sieves, knives, spoons, wooden bowls, camp pails, brass kettles, clam shells, and Indian trinkets. We made a selection and placed them in the back end of our wagon.

The enriched soil about the ruins was nourishing grass of a swampy height, and the purslain plant was growing rank and tender. We picked a large quantity of it to boil for greens.

On our return home made a call at an Indian trading house, or an Indian chief's house, now going to decay. But it looked quite live-like, and if we had it here at the Settlement, should think we had a good house to live in. There too the grass was growing a monstrous growth, and snuggling down close to the ground were a "power" of spotted liz-ards making their abode in the cool dense woods of

grass. Have had some of our purslain greens boiled
for dinner to-day, and though seasoned with nothing
but salt, they relished well with our Johnny-cake.

Mother has set herself to work scouring up our
plunder of the thrown away Indian utensils—so now
we shall have quite an addition to our kitchen ware.
Father has stowed away the pieces of buffalo skin
in the loft, close up in under the eaves, to be handy
when strings are needed.

CHAPTER V.

Here is an Eden garden land,
Where nature, with a profuse hand
Has clustered beauties rich and fair,
That will with fairy land compare.

Shall free-men stand upon her soil
And elevate the true man's toil?
Or chains that clank, and fetters dark
Crush down that pure and noble spark?

The clash of arms is on the air—
The soil is wet with bloody gore—
O God, behold in power and might!
Defend the true—protect the right!

JUNE 14TH.—The disappointment in the company,
the unsettled state of the Territory, the distance from
my own native land, and premonitions of greater
trouble, all combine to make me sad and sorrowful
in this far-off land. My Willie saw me weeping to-
day; he asked, "What ails mamma?" I told him,
"Mamma wants to go back to her old home." He
then said, "Mamma, ain't the flowers pretty?"

Sweet child! he is happy among the flowers, and thinks his mamma need not feel bad where there are so many pretty flowers.

My two precious children have not made the least complaint about hard fare, or even asked why they do not have the comforts they have been used to having. They have their tin cups filled with bouquets of fresh flowers every day. Innocent and trusting childhood; sipping enjoyment like bees, wherever it can be found.

Mr. Buxton has returned from Kansas City, where he went after Mr. Stewart's household goods. While passing Westport, the northern invaders came upon him, took his horses from his wagon, and were proceeding to examine his boxes of goods, expecting to find Sharp's rifles. He was obliged to flee for his life, leaving wagon and goods to the mercy of Border Ruffianism. He had letters for members of the company, which he dared not keep about his person— tore them up and threw them away—putting the money into his boots which had been sent by different members to purchase articles that could not be found in Kansas City—took a round-about way, and has now arrived safely in the Settlement.

No papers are allowed to come into the Territory. We hear that the merciless mob have sacked the new city of Lawrence, and destroyed the fast growing town of Osawatomie—entering houses, taking and destroying everything that came in their way, demanding rings from women's fingers, and jewels from their ears! They are threatening destruction to this small Settlement. We keep our trunks packed and locked, and I am made treasurer of funds and valuables, which I keep secreted about my person. We lie down in fear at night, and arise in the morning expecting to see the mob approching.

May Heaven grant that after all the trials and fears of a pioneer life which we are striving to live above, we may not fall into the hands of a Border Ruffian, drunken, ruthless mob.

Mr. V. has mown some prairie grass, and we have filled our straw ticks with it; find it an improvement in our dormitory. I am obliged to make my bed up crosswise of the tick, to give four of us a chance. It makes the bed plenty long enough for the children, but my husband and I have some difficulty in lodging our extremities. Mrs. V. and myself have the arrangement of the loft all to ourselves, now that Dr. House and Mr. Sober are gone. The two wagon boards are given to sister L. to improve her lodgings. Her boards are supported by trunks, leaving them free in the middle for quite a spring.

JUNE 15TH.—Church at Mr. Clubb's. This is a bright, lovely, quiet Sabbath day; surely, a Sabbath serenity is diffused over all. All nature is silently praising the Divine Upholder; and shall we not praise Him too? though with a saddened tone. The air is sweet and pure now, and a mild breeze is blowing from the southwest. Others have written of a vitality in the atmosphere of Kansas that is truly wonderful, "it breathes new life around, and vigor and buoyancy is felt coming back to old limbs." My health has not been so good for years, as since I have been in the Territory; my headaches have lost the greater share of their severity, and I feel equal for any task. I never was so thin in flesh, and never felt such agility.

The fever and ague has been called by some, the "emigrant's bug-bear," by others, the "real bear." But no bears of that kind come growling around us yet. May we be spared, also, from *its* fever and ague shaking powers.

We have sunsets now that will do to look upon. The large, crimsoned, wheel-like sun approaches the horizon leaving not a cloud to be goldened; but the whole western sky is enriched with his hue, until he is swallowed up without twilight in the depths beyond where the tall grass keeps waving, and night shuts out the splendid view.

Kansas moons have been described as equaling Italy's moons in loveliness. What Italy's moons are I know not by experienco, but the moons here are lovely far beyond describing words. The "pale Empress of night" floats up into the blue sky studded with golden gems, with her milky drapery on, bending the zenith almost down with her pure robes. The gentle acclivity, the slowly declining prairie swell, the deep ravine, the white arms of the Sycamore, the drooping willow, the dry oak, the rich flowers and pearly dew, all reflect with angel purity her soft, mellow, and fleecy light. Who can look on scenes like these, without being bathed to the spirits care with a feeling of holy adoration and ardent prayer to God?

> "In the walks of life, wherever
>   They may lead, tho' dark or fair—
> In the forest, on the highway,
>   Ever keep a heart of prayer;
> Thou wilt find it a consoling,
>   All-sustaining guardian here—
> 'Tis the master-key of Heaven!
>   *Pure*, confiding, ardent prayer."

June 16th.—What are we to look for, and what fear next? The mosquitoes have come upon us all of a sudden. They troubled us very much at the creek to-day while washing. After washing, Mrs. V and myself went down the creek into the embowered bottom lands to refresh ourselves with a bathe, and the mosquitoes came in such swarms upon us that we thought they would carry us off by tit-bits before we could protect ourselves with our clothing. I don't see for my part where Max Greene kept himself in this country, when he says, (speaking of mosquitoes,) "And away from Kansas river there are none—none, at all events, that ever presented their bills to me." From the high idea I have formed of him, I certainly can't think him wanting in flavor. Our bed being short, in the night they

6

have a good chance to nibble away at our protruding extremities. I lie awake—I can't sleep for their music and the pain and inflammation caused by their bites. I try to keep my children covered, so they wont eat them all up before morning. As for myself, I get so infuriated that I get up, descend the ladder, make my way out into the wet grass upon the run, not minding what reptiles may be under my bare feet; I then return from my dewy bath, lie down and try to sleep, but it is almost in vain.

JUNE 17TH.—The soil of rich layers of vegetable mould, is throwing up the rows of dark green blades of corn. Our cornfield of six acres looks promising, as do all cornfields around. Pumpkins, squashes, melons, cucumbers, beans, pease, potatoes, and tomatoes are thriving finely. The next work our settlers will find to do, will be fencing cornfields, splitting rails, cutting poles, and drawing them from the bottom lands to do it with. Mr. Clubb intends to commence his house soon, which is to be built of the soft stone, that is found here, that can be cut in any shape, and hardens on exposure to the air. He has a fine site for his house on one of the prairie billows, a little out from the timber, where dame nature has lined his avenues with spreading oaks, arched his gateways with hickory and vines, and clumped around his (*airy*) dwelling, the sweet walnut, wild rose, and many a floral gem.

There are endless beds of coal in this region, underlying the soil, cropping out here and there, assuring the squatter sovereign that he need not go cold in winter, if he will just dig for coal.

The lime-stone, too, heaves out into ledges on the ridges, speaking in a natural language, that though there is a scarcity of timber in this beautiful country, nature has provided many a substitute—and that with the soft building stone, and plenty of mortar, nice and comfortable houses can be built.

JUNE 21ST.—Baking day, and hominy pudding day come here every day, so that a great share of my time is spent in the large kitchen. I tended the boiling hominy, and baked a good Johnny-cake this forenoon. Now one of my white loaves is out of the Dutch oven, and the other is baking; it will soon be done. The old people think the fare here is hard, and so it is, for them—they don't want to eat anything made of corn; and where we shall get the next flour, I know not; it will be very high, wherever we find it.

I live entirely on food made of corn—hominy and milk and Johnny-cake and milk—and try to persuade the children to, leaving the wheat bread for grandma and grand-pa. To-day, at dinner, I told Willie mamma had got some good Johnny-cake, and asked him to have some in his milk. He said, "Willie *rather have white bread;*" and the little fellow will eat it clear, and relish it much better than children with pampered appetites do their round of goodies. O! come all you children who have parta-

ken of your good things, until they are lying in waste
around you—come and behold my darling boy, sitting on his little round log, for want of a chair,
smacking his lips over a piece of white bread, and
learn the real value there is in *a piece of white
bread!*

As far as diet is concerned, the simple diet I get
here agrees with my system well, and what shall *I*
eat? is the least of all that troubles me; but to see
the old people wanting for comforts they have been
accustomed to, and fear that I may see them all doing with still less comforts, touches a chord in my
heart of feeling.

SUNDAY, JUNE 22D.—My husband and self have
been spending some of the hours of this Sabbath-
day in writing to our good friends away in the northern land. We have given them a description of this
"fairy land;" thought we would not trouble them
with any disclosures of disappointments, etc; for we
mean to live above and outgrow them, make us a
home in this sunny south, garlanded with vines,
embossed around with many flowers, and wearing
the halo of true and loving hearts. Have received
a letter from St. Louis, stating that our household
goods have arrived in that place; my husband feels
very anxious now to get his cabin built, so as to go to
Kansas City for them, when they shall have arrived
there. We are wanting, *now*, the bushel of dried
apple our boxes contain, and the children are wish-

ing they had some of "mamma's dried berries."
Have been to the spring with my husband for water;
our spring is getting dry, as are all the springs near
here; we must then go to the creek for water. While
returning from the spring, we set down our pails,
and amused ourselves with the grasshoppers. I
thought of the riddle I used to read in my little
primer,

> "Long legs laughless,
> Come up to the door staffless,
> More afraid of cock and hen,
> Than of dog and twenty men."

I never saw so many kinds and sizes of grasshoppers as I see in this land, from hopping to flying;
some small, some two or three inches in length, and
looking more like pieces of the stalk of prairie grass,
with their green thread-like legs hopping about, than
anything else; and so they are from that size up to
the size of a decent frog; I can easily understand
now, how it is that the Indians are said to live sometimes on grasshoppers, for one would make a good
mouthful, after being skinned and hung up.

It is rumored this evening that one of the Ohio
men has had a fit of the fever and ague to-day.
Hope it may not be so.

The children ask permission to go a little way
from the cabin, to get what they call pieces of yellow paper; upon reaching them, find they are
large yellow evening primroses, just bursting at

this evening hour into bloom. They grow on a stalk much lower than those we cultivate at home, but the flower is as large as a hollyhock.

> " When once the sun sinks in the west,
>   And dew-drops pearl the evening's breast ;
>   Almost as pale as moonbeams are,
>   Or its companionable star,
>   The evening primrose opes anew
>   Its delicate blossoms to the dew ;
>   And, hermit-like, shunning the light,
>   Wastes its fair bloom upon the night."

June 23d.—Father and my husband have been off east upon Big Creek, looking claims. No one about here knows of the untaken claims there. They say that when settlers come in this fall, they will sell their land here, and take claims there. My husband says, "The scenery is lovely, far surpassing the scenery here on the Neosho. It is higher, and the prospect more beautiful—the water is clear, and the creek never dry"—and that he will write to some of our northern friends to come and settle beside us.

We have been giving attention to the description of Big Creek—but now, at the commencement of this lovely eve, we are sitting about our cabin door —grand-pa and grand-ma seated on the high threshhold, the rest of us on stones—Willie climbing on to his papa's lap—Mema stands by my side—all listening to the song of one lone whippowil, which comes up from some shady dell by the river's side. The thousands of frogs now break in with their melodies, from the soprano peeper, up to the bass "grout"— and here, too, come swarms of mosquitoes about our ears, with their "cousining" chorus, which we are trying to drive away with smoke.

CHAPTER VI.

From premonic clouds begin to flow
    The drops that have been gathering there,
They may fall fast, or they may come slow ;
    Our heads must bow now, to take their share.

Disease is shaking our frames with cold—
    High fever comes, writhing each limb with pain,
The cheeks crimsoned—in the temples fold
    Wild imaginings of loss or gain.

The raiment is wet with sallow dew,
    The eye glistens no longer with hope,
The food is all bitterness to chew,
    And in weakness to water they'll grope.

JUNE 26TH.—Several members of our company
have suddenly been taken with the chills and fever ;
and here in our own cabin it has fallen upon Mr. V.
and wife, mother, sister L. and Mema. It is sorrowful to see what a change comes over them in one
day. Mr. V. thinks this is too much for him to
stand—will leave cornfield, and all the prospects of
this beautiful country, and hasten to the North
again, if this is the way new settlers have to be

shaken in this "sunny" land. He will make arrangements with the first team going to Kansas City, to be taken there. In my opinion, we shall find this disease to be no "bugbear," but shall feel that the white Greenlander, the real "hugger," has got us in his embrace.

JUNE 29TH.—A lovely Sunday. I, too, have fallen victim to the dreaded disease. Mr. and Mrs. V., Mema and myself, have occupied the loft to-day. Dishes of water have been set near our heads, so that we could help ourselves to drink when it seemed as though we should burn up with fever. My head has ached dreadfully; am glad to crawl down the ladder, with weakened limbs get out door here, sit down on a stone, lean my dizzy head against the logs of the cabin, breathe a little fresh air, see the sun go down, and ask, "can this be the same sun that shines upon our Northern friends, who are enjoying blessings and comforts they know not how to appreciate?"

JUNE 30TH.—Mr. V. has spoken for a passage in an ox-wagon, for himself and wife, to Kansas City; and my husband thinks we had better make preparations to leave the Territory with him, and not wait till he and father get sick; so he has done the washing to-day himself, and packed our trunks. And now, since our paroxysms of chills and fever went off for the day, sister L. has packed their

trunks, and I have been trying to help my husband
cook a little to take on our journey Northward. I
have mixed up some bread, using baking powder for
risings, for I could not tend to raising yeast. I find
myself very weak—was obliged to sit down twice
while mixing my bread. When I began to feel faint
and dizzy, I would sit down on a stone, and when
the dizziness passed off, go on with my mixing.

My husband is now baking the bread in the Dutch
oven. This is the first lesson he has taken in baking
in my big kitchen, and it troubles him to keep the
coals on the oven. I believe we shall be ready to
start any time now, when the command is given.

It requires but little preparation for "squatters"
to be ready to start on a journey. The bag of corn
meal and Dutch oven are stowed handily by in the
back end of the wagon, and the wooden tray to mix
in; so when halting time comes, a fire is kindled,
the cooking utensils sally forth and begin service.

JULY 1ST.—The water is fast drying up; the spring
that was cleaned out and dug deeper, in the gulch
below our cabin, is almost dry; the water is not fit
to drink.

Disappointment is on the approach again! Am
afraid father is going to upset all of our calculations
about getting away. He declares, out and out, that
he will not go. Mother and sister L. have been very
anxious to leave the country; have tried to persuade
father that it was best to go—so has my husband;

but his indomitable will is not thus to be turned. He has gone nine miles, to Godfrey's, to-day, to learn the whereabouts of a living spring of water, that is said to be near the old Indian trading house.

I have missed my chill to-day; the others are suffering severely. My Mema complains of her head's aching very hard through her temples, and seems to be almost burning up with fever; calls for water, water, and I have no good water to give her, or the others.

JULY 2D.—"A doomed ship!" thought I, this morning, as father unceremoniously yoked the oxen, put them before the wagon, placed in mother's bed, their trunks, some provisions and cooking utensils, told mother and Lydia to get in, and said, "I am going to the old Indian house, where I can get some water to drink!"

About noon the man came for Mr. V. and wife, to take them to his cabin until he should be ready to start for Kansas City. Mr. V. is so weak and feeble, that my husband had to help him into the wagon. After they were gone, I sat my weak self to sweeping out, for it left some spare room where mother's bed had stood in the corner, and where six trunks had been setting along around. Then I made ready our simple supper, in time my husband should return, after following the old people on foot to their new abiding place, to see how they got there, and take the oxen and wagon back. Ate supper with my husband and two children alone, for the first time since we left our comfortable Northern home. This difficult question comes up now to be answered: "What shall we do?" To leave the Territory is impossible; and to me it seems like going into utter darkness to go up to that old Indian house. There we shall be four miles from neighbors, and on the Indian lands too. If they should return from their hunt and find us there, they would think we were intruding almost too much, and I know not what our fate might be. We cannot stay here without water, neither can we leave the old people four miles away, alone, to do without milk, (for it is all we have to make our food palatable.) We conclude that we must submit to the dominion of paternity, and take the result.

JULY 3D.—The hot summer's sun of this climate is drying up the fountains of water, pouring his scorching rays upon us, unobstructed by a cloud, and visiting us with a disease that is *paling* almost every face, and crippling the limbs with weakness! I am alone with my children; my husband is getting out fencing. My Mema's chill has passed off, and she is in a raging fever. Mr. H. S. Clubb is sick with a fever. He has just passed by in a wagon; he is being taken ten miles away upon the higher prairie; thinks the air may be freer from miasma, and unfailing water is to be found there. Father Cosgrove and two young men are sick at Mr. Adams'; several boarders at Mr. Stewart's are also sick.

JULY 4TH.—To-day the sun comes pouring down his floods of heat again. I can't step outside the cabin door without burning my feet. The prairie grass makes such a wear and tear upon our shoe leather, that I am trying to save my own calf-skin shoes, for I see that they are being worn badly now, and I shall want them more when cold weather comes; so I go barefoot inside, and slip my feet into my rubbers when I go from the cabin. Husband meets father at the cornfield to get out fencing.

The Ohio brothers, with their wives, started off this morning for Kansas City; they are going back to Ohio. I watched the white top of the wagon, while with slow and firm tread the oxen were wading through the tall grass, and bearing it away like a ship at sea, over the billowy prairie ocean. It finally became like a white speck this side of the blue sky, and then was gone. A sigh must escape, a tear fall, a wish be breathed that our wagon was in the rear, with all our family in it. But destiny! destiny! *inexorable destiny!* has bound us.

My darling Willie was taken sick after his papa went to the cornfield; I found two scantling-like pieces of wood, which I placed on to our stone floor, laid across some of the "shakes," and spread thereon Indian blankets for a bed for my two sick children; I could not have them in the loft, to climb so many times up and down the ladder. Willie has been in a high fever; I have given him water and baths.

This is a most unhappy day, and a still, sad Fourth. I have tried to write a letter home, but cannot write; my thoughts are away where friends are all life and enjoyment; but it only darkens the gloom that envelopes all my hopes!

It is night now; my husband has returned from his work; he feels cold and almost sick; I make for him a rare treat, a cup of tea! and he sits drinking it out of a tin cup. I hope he will feel better.

July 5th.—My husband is not well to-day; cannot meet father at the cornfield. Mema and Willie have both got their chills—the fever will soon come rushing on. I feel weak, very weak, myself, but must keep up; think I shall not have any more of the paroxysms, for the disease was well worn out with me in my youth, on the borders of Lake Champlain.

July 6th.—A hard thunder storm was upon us this morning, which kept us in bed, in our damp bed, until about ten o'clock—that being the dryest place we could find. Everything was drenched with water; our fireplace was one complete mortar bed. I chanced to have a few chips up one side of our cabin that were dry; of these I made a fire in an old tin pan, strung a tea kettle on to the broom handle, making one end fast between the logs of the cabin, while my husband held the other, and over that fire in the pan I made Graham pudding for our breakfast.

Mr. Adams came, milked the cow, fed the calf, and brought some water from the creek.

My husband feels cold and sick. I have been to Mr. Adams' for some ginger; my strength almost failed me on my way there and back, but he has got the ginger tea; hope he will feel better.

JULY 7TH.—Found no improvement in health this morning. Neighbor Adams came, loaded our trunks, bed, and few cooking utensils into our wagon, tied our cow behind, leaving the calf to frolic at its pleasure; we then seated ourselves inside and started for the Indian house. William gave the oxen the "rein;" they took their own time, and made their own way. As we passed the cornfield, saw the corn was growing finely, and I wanted to get out and pick another mess of green pease, but a large yellow wolf was stretching up his head, gazing upon us from the middle of the field where the pease were growing, so I dared not make the attempt. When we arrived here, found mother and sister L. having their chills; my children had been taken with theirs on the way.

Father unloaded the wagon, I made up our bed on the floor in the east room, mother has hers in the west room. A fire place in each room, no glass in the windows, but doors opening on to a piazza on the north side. This old dilapidated house, as rude as it is, is a palace to the rude cabin we have left.

I see by the dish of boiled greens on the rough, bench-like table in one corner, that father has been to the purslain beds at the wigwam ruins.

Father has tied the cow to an oak bush near, the calf to another, where they can eat from the deep grass. He has left the yoke on the oxen, and will watch them lest they stray away, and chain them to the wagon at night.

Father has been to the spring, which he says is one-half mile away, descending towards the bottom lands; there it comes issuing from a rocky hillside, in all its sparkling, chilly purity. It is, indeed, a priceless treasure in this hot climate, and to fever-parched lips, and throbbing temples, it is life.

JULY 8TH.—My husband started off with oxen and wagon this morning for Mr. Stewart's, six miles away, after some corn meal that he had bought. He looked pale and feeble; did not like to see him go alone, but could not leave the sick ones to go with him. Father is preparing some wood; I am baking bread by the *fireplace*, and taking care of four sick ones.

Day is on the decline; I have been looking in the direction of the settlement for the appearance of the white-topped wagon. Father says, "it will come in between the lines of trees yonder." The children are up now, out here on the piazza with their pale faces, watching with me, to see the wagon come in between the trees. The west is crimsoned with a glorious sunset, the sun's rich rays are painting the high grass as it waves to and fro; the random clumps of oak bushes multitudinously scattered around this rude dwelling, are bathed in his radiance; and he gives lustre to the pale faces, who fear they shall not see husband or papa to-night. The sun is down. The rays blinded our eyes so that we could not see the wagon, as it came in between the trees. My husband says he had a chill, and was obliged to go to bed at Mr. Stewart's, until his fever was off some, before he could start to come back. Has rode, lying down, all the way.

Our true oxen are deserving of much approbation, and shall receive a kind pat for bringing safely to our rude lodgings, one so dearly loved.

JULY 9TH.—All sick to-day, but father and myself! Father has been to the spring with the oxen and wagon; has drawn all the water he could in our shallow storage. I have washed and taken care of five sick ones, they all calling for water! water! at the same time.

7

CHAPTER VII.

ALL SICK BUT MYSELF, ETC.

"Let faith suppress each rising fear,
    Each anxious doubt exclude;
Thy Maker's will hath placed thee here—
    A Maker wise and good!

He to thy every trial knows
    Its just restraint to give;
Attentive to behold thy woes,
    And faithful to relieve.

Then why thus heavy, O my soul!
    Say, why distrustful still;
Thy thoughts with vain impatience roll
    O'er scenes of future ill?

Though griefs unnumbered throng thee round,
    Still in thy God confide,
Whose finger marks the seas their bound,
    And curbs the headlong tide."

JULY 13TH.—Father's name is now added to the list of the sick. How can I stay this flood of tears, as I look about and see all but myself prostrated with sickness? so pale and weak, and amid so many discomforts. It is impossible for me to do for them as they require. I am weak myself; it seems when I go for water that I can never get back again. Have just been to the spring for my turn of water, one-half mile, which I bring in a six quart camp-pail and Indian coffee pot of the same dimensions. It is all the way up hill from the spring. This is a long, long Sabbath day. I look north, south, east and west, from this pinnacle of prairie, away where the green and blue blend together; nobody can I see, and nothing can I hear, save the cow and calf nipping the grass by the oak bushes. Even little Sambo dog is as still as death, near where my Willie boy is sleeping, in his high fever. This is solitude —anxious, fearful solitude! *"O, God, forsake us not utterly!"*

JULY 16TH.—Yesterday morning, father drove out to the settlement before his chill came on, and drove back last eve, after his fever was off. He went to see if he could get some one to stay with us for a few days. Our good neighbor, Mr. Stewart, sent his hired man, Mr. Buxton, this morning. He prepares wood, takes care of the oxen, cow and calf, and brings water. I have been writing to friends, sitting on the floor, with my portfolio on a cracker box for a writing desk. My husband is lying on our bed of prairie grass, on the floor; his fever is passing off. Willie lies on an Indian blanket near the door, calling for water. Mother lies on her bed in the other room; seems very sick. Father on a

blanket, on the floor; his fever is raging. Lydia
has got up and is sitting on her trunk; looks weak
and sad. Mema's fever is off; she is out beside the
house, amusing herself by picking up Indian beads
that are washed up from the dirt, with the drippings
from the eaves when it rains. Mr. B. has gone for
some good, cold water. Just three months to-day
since we left home; mark the contrast!

JULY 18TH.—It became necessary for me to go to
the settlement to-day. The children were so anxious to go with me, that I spread blankets on to the
wagon floor for them to lie on, hung the covered tin
pail of water to one of the bows, to quench their
feverish thirst when it should come on; and with
Mrs. B. driving, we started off. Went six miles, to
Mr. Stewart's, did my business, took dinner, had my
children rest on a bed, borrowed a sieve, and then
returned home in season to look after the wants of
the sick left alone. I had a chill yesterday, and to-
day on my return; feel weak, but must go and sift
some meal to make a pudding for our supper. I
have been obliged to make the pudding of unsifted
meal since we have been here; think we shall notice
the difference to-night.

JULY 20TH.—Mr. Stewart and his good lady have
been to see us to-day. It was indeed refreshing to
see such kind-hearted people; they cheered my husband, while they hoped better times for us all.

This is the first company we have had to serve since we came into the Territory. I boiled some rice from our scanty store, gave them a little sugar to eat on it, and had some cold hominy and milk. They ate the plain refreshments I had for them, standing by the rude Indian table in one corner, just large enough for two to stand by. No apologies were necessary, no ceremony in serving was expected; we are dealing with the sad realities of life.

JULY 25TH.—This has been a very hot day, as are all the days now. We are so high up here, that it seems as though we were in close proximity to the king of day, and near the seat of the monarch of the storm. Two terrific storms have come upon us of late; in a moment the sky would blacken, the thunder-clouds burst, the heavens be set on fire with lightning, and the rain pour down like water spouts. It seems as though the bowels of the earth, after every clap of thunder, must be our precipitation, Indian house and all. But we are better sheltered from the storms here than at the settlement. Their anger soon vents its fury, the sky is cleared of every remnant of clouds, and the myriads of suspended water drops glisten in the sun's bright rays.

Mr. Buxton has been taken sick, and gone home, which leaves me to do all. I chain the oxen to the wagon that stands before the door nights, and keep them chained till eleven o'clock in the forenoon; I then give them their liberty; they go directly to the spring to drink, then into the shady bottom lands, and feed until a little after sundown; I then hear them come rushing through the oak bushes, in their yoke, to the house. Their return home at night is very welcome, as it ceases my anxiety about them; their heavy breathing, and the clanking of their captive chain, is much company all through the long, lonely, and to me, almost sleepless nights. The cow and calf I keep tied to the oak bushes, changing them after they have eaten the grass in a circle around, the length of their rope. I lead the cow to the spring every morning to drink, and lead the calf to the cow every time I milk, for it to take its warm, rich meal. I give it dish water for drink—it is almost too bad, but then, it is such hard work for me to bring water.

I was all out of wood to-day; did not know what to do, there being no wood about that I could pick up, when suddenly a man came in; he was ragged and dirty; seemed very strange, and said but little; asked for victuals; I told him to cut some wood and I would give him some. He cut the wood, ate his victuals, and vanished. I know not which way he came, or which way he went.

JULY 27TH.—Another long, lonely, and silent Sabbath day! The sick are lying about upon their beds and blankets, uncomplainingly—just calling for water, water! I have looked, and looked, to see if I could see a white-topped wagon coming in between the trees. But no wagon do I see,—no sound do I hear in the distance, and nothing near save the mourning dove, who comes every day and repeats its sad lay of O-o-o! O-o-o! O-o-o! on the roof of the house, chiming in well with the breathings of my own heart.

> "But if pity inspire thee, renew the sad lay."

I feel that here I am in the charnel house of the red men's bones! for all around, all over these prairies, can be seen the monuments of the Indian's grave,—quite a number just back of the house, but of ancient burial. The Indians here dig a very shallow grave, build up around it a little pen, "cob-house fashion," of logs, put the body in, in a blanket, put over the buffalo robe and a slight covering of dirt, so slight that the robe has been lifted and the body seen. If it is an Indian of note, his pony is slain, and it, and all that belongs to him, share with him his grave,—and with him, his heaven.

> "His soul-proud science never taught to stray
> Far as the Solar Walk, or Milky Way,
> Yet, simple nature to his hope has given,
> Behind the cloud-topt hills, a humbler heav'n;
> Some safer world in depth of woods embrac'd,
> Some happier island in the watery waste;
> Where slaves once more their native land behold,
> No fiends torment, no Christians thirst for gold.
> To BE. contents his natural desire;
> He asks no angel's wing, no seraph's fire;
> But thinks, admitted to that equal sky,
> His faithful dog shall bear him company."

I take little Sambo dog with me sometimes, when
I go for water; for his pat, pat, pat, along in the
path behind me, is another sound added to my own
tread; he is really a great deal of company for me,
makes the way seem much shorter, and when I come
right upon a great rattlesnake in my path, I step
out, hasten along, without looking around to see
how Sambo gets by; but soon again hear his pat at
my heels,—then know he is safely past.

A day or two since, sister L. called me to see what
it was that was laying its shiny head on the threshhold of the door between our rooms, while its body
was concealed under the floor. I saw, at once, it
was the head of a copper-head snake; I caught my
India-rubber, the first thing within my reach, and
gave it one blow on the head, which it instantly drew
in under the floor, but not without leaving a mark.
I have seen no more of it.

We frequently see rattlesnakes crawling and hanging over the sills under the piazza where the floor is
up. We hear a peculiar noise under the floor sometimes, have thought it was rats, but find it is the
noise of snakes. My husband keeps a long hickory
cane lying on the bed, so that when he hears that
peculiar noise, he strikes on the floor near where
some of the floor boards are gone, to drive the snakes
away. But there is no dread of the vemom of
snakes to me,—I wish that was all that made me
fear.

There is a snake that infests this country, called

the blow snake; when startled it blows its venom
out upon the air, causing stupefaction and death.
The large, gray, mountain rattlesnake has been seen
by father, near our cornfield, several feet in length;
and black snakes have been seen yards in length,
swimming in the creeks.

The tarantula, a venomous spider, has been found
taking up its abode between the barks of some of our
settlers' cabins.

JULY 29TH.—Kind Providence sent that mysterious person here again to-day; his red shirt sleeves
were more ragged than before. As before, I could
not learn from him which way he came, or which
way or where he was going. He was hungry. I
gave him something to eat, and asked him to chop
what wood was at the door; after which he started
off east over the prairies.

Have been taking some of the sick ones out to ride
to-day; was surprised to find that the oxen would
mind me when I said "whoa!" "gee!" and "haw!"
My husband complimented me upon my tact, in my
first attempt at driving oxen.

Coarser kinds of flowers now blossom on the prairies, than the rich, lively, and delicate of June; yellow flowers in fields, from the size of a daisy up to
the large aspiring sunflower. They seem to vie with
the sun for golden splendor. Many of the stalks of
these summer flowers are thick and juicy, nature
fitting them for the dry and intense heat of the sea-

son. Varieties of the cactus family are grouped
here and there where the grass is not so high; and
the resin weed by the path side, which conceals tur-
pentine, will let you know on being broken.

Been to the spring five times to-day; three times
is my usual number for going; but when I am storing some for slop washing (which by the way is all
the washing we have done here) I go five times, making five miles' travel for me to bring sixty quarts
of water. For the last turn, I go just at sunset, to
get some to the house cool, for bringing it so far in
the heat of the day, it gets warm before I can place
it to the fevered lips; I being the only one to enjoy
a cold draught at the fountain, which gives life and
strength upon these hot days.

When at the spring, at the close of the day, I
hear the howl of wolves a little below in the bottom
lands, soon hear their answering howl in multiplied
numbers, all around, all over the prairies. I sometimes fear they will surround me, and "take *care* of
me," before I can reach the house.

JULY 31ST.—This is my husband's fortieth birth-
day. I have never seen him so sick since our path-
ways run together, hardly ever lost a day; yet his
frame is slender; he has always made it a work of
conscience to take care of the physical—to be tem-
perate in all things. A deeper sadness comes over
me as I review, to-day, the many bright spots and
sunny hours that have flowed with enjoyment, unto

us who have always been happy in each other's society, and contrast with our present dark surroundings. My husband has his chill and fever now in the night. I sit up with him, give him vapor baths when the chill is on, and towel baths in his fever; he thinks he will be well in a few days; he is sitting up, and he and father are building our log cabin in imagination. I am sorry my hope is so small—can't see why we should improve much in health at present, when the air is so loaded with miasma, mornings, that it broods over us in its density a long time, and smells as though it had just made its escape from a field of decaying cabbage.

Last night our oxen came not to the house at the usual time. I watched and listened at intervals, until it was getting late, to hear them breaking the oak brushes in their way up to the house; but they came not. The night was long, and seemed so very still and lonely without their company. My husband felt anxious; he feared they had gone towards the Settlement and would get into his cornfield, destroy the corn, and eat so much as to kill themselves. This morning I told him I wanted to go to the Settlement to see if they were there; he told me which trail to take, to lead me to the cornfield, then I knew the way. When one mile from here I mistook, and took the wrong trail, there being so many checkering the prairie. I walked a long way before I discovered my mistake, then thought I must be nearly parallel with the right one, and would keep on and

soon come out at the cornfield. The trail led me
down into a quiet dell shaded by the sycamore, oak,
and black walnut, while the branches of the latter
were dropping continually at my feet their large,
yellow and precocious nuts; and along close by
murmured the little brook over its pebbly falls. The
scene was enchanting, and if I had had time, and
happiness had dwelt within, could have taken long
sips of pure inspiration. I thought, here the wild
man and maiden have sat perchance, and breathed
into each other's ear their simple lay of love,—here
made vows, and here rested, until yonder sun shot
his rays aslant the green bower above, and the little
brook murmured its eloquence to the dewy eve. I
passed this enchanting nook and came out into large
fields of what I would call at once, cultivated grain.
This wild grain was waving its heads in silence high
above my own, and extending acres and acres away.
The trail led through,—but felt that I was too much
out of my way to come out right. So I retraced
my steps—then crossing through the tall grass, almost swamping myself from trail to trail; could not
persuade myself that I was on the right track. I
have returned to the old Indian house without finding the oxen, and am very tired. My husband feels
disappointed that I did not find my way. I tell him
I will rise early in the morning, and if there is but
little dew, will be off in time, to try my luck again.

Aug. 1st.—Fulfilled my promise in rising early;

milked, waited upon calfie to its early meal, led the cow to the spring, made a pudding for breakfast, took mine, hurried away leaving my children still asleep, and the others to get up and take care of themselves. By six o'clock I was out on the damp prairie—found where two trails had united ; I had taken the left instead of the right. Followed on, and as I began to descend on to the lower prairie, found plenty of wet grass, and was glad my costume was so well adapted to my long, dewy, morning walk. As I neared the cornfield, could see signs of our oxen there. Went on to Mr. Adams'. They said that they had seen nothing of them; I then knew they had gone east toward Missouri, and that I must go to Mr. Stewart's, to see if he could find some one to go and look for them. At Mr. Adams' I found the elder Broadbent ; said he was going up to the Indian house to see us ; I thanked him for his kindness in making the attempt, told him which trail to take after he had passed the cornfield, and to go and keep them company until I should return. Went on to Mr. Stewart's. Found him making fence a little this side of his cabin; told him my business ; he said he would attend to it; and bade me go to the cabin, rest myself and get some dinner. After dinner he told Mr. Blackburn, one of our company, (whose family was still east,) to take the large horse for himself, and the pony that the women folks ride, for me ; to go back with me, and then go and look for the open.

I mounted the pony on a man's saddle, and we started off; but it had been so long since I had practiced riding horse-back, and never on a man's saddle, that I could make but very little headway; I felt in a great hurry to get back to my family, for they would need me, and the children would make many inquiries about mamma; so when out of sight of the cabin a little, riding through a large field of tall wild sunflowers all in bloom, I told Mr. B. that I never should get home at such a slow rate, and that I must conform to circumstances, so if he would just ride along a little in advance, I would soon arrange myself to keep up with him; having on my Bloomer with calico pants, I just put a foot into each *stirrup*, then putting the skirt of my Bloomer all modestly down, rode up alongside of my companion. He made no remark, and like a gentleman, as he was, never seemed to notice my position. But it was surprising to me, to see with what ease, safety, and speed, I could now ride horse-back! I *was just following the fashion* of the native women of the country—that was all! In a short time six miles had vanished, and we were nearing this, our place of abode. My husband's fever was leaving him; he lay out on the piazza on an Indian blanket; he smiled as he saw me alight, saying, "Why, Miriam, what will you do next?"

Found father Broadbent visiting with father; he went with me to the spring to help bring water, and as we walked to and from, he tried to comfort me—

good old man! with the bright prospects he could see in advance for us, in this beautiful country.

I have nursed up the sick ones, and petted and comforted my children, and we have all refreshed ourselves with our simple meal. Have given father Broadbent an Indian blanket, with a pillow, and told him where to spread it; I am now through with another anxious day; am "weary and heavy laden," will spread my blanket out here on the piazza, and if there is wind enough to blow away the clouds of mosquitoes that hatch and come from the deep grass, I think I can sleep some.

Oh! Father in Heaven, strengthen all our hearts for what we shall be compelled to undergo; may we feel that it is divine influence that impels us on— may we remember that thy loving kindness and tender mercies are over all thy works, and to thee, O God! do I look in these dark days. Refresh to-night with balmy sleep.

CHAPTER VIII.

INDIANS RETURN FROM HUNT, ETC.

Hark! the token of the red man's approach
Breaks on my ear, my heart with trembling beats!
A herald comes with lightning-speed, all on
A courser white,—and says, "Wau-shau—she's come!
Their anger burns that white men should intrude."
Away! while 'Spirit Great,' him in sleep doth bind.
"What shall we do?" I'll fly for help to come,
To save all those for whom I live and love,
Though dangers my pathway be girt around.
O God! from us this awful doom avert!"

SUNDAY, AUGUST 3D.—Yesterday morning, I rose feeling another premonic pressure upon me; my heart was trembling with fear again. Mr. Blackburn returned from Godfrey's, said our oxen had been there, and a man was sent to "take them up," but they run faster than he could, so he gave up, leaving them running away as fast as they could, east toward the Catholic Mission. Mr. B. not being used to traveling on the prairie, my husband agreed with him to find some one that was, and send right on after the oxen. Mr. B. and father Broadbent then left for the Settlement, leaving us again alone.

I went about my daily work, caring for the sick and weak; went to the spring for water; while gone, thought I heard dogs bark over across the river, told my husband what I heard, saying, "I am sure the Indians have returned from their hunt. All of this yelping, growling and barking, as though the dog kennels were all upturned, can't come from wolves in the day-time; it must proceed from the scores of long, lank, peaked-nosed, gray, and half starved Indian dogs!" He said it could not be, they were not expected until nearly the first of September, and tried to quiet my fears by saying that we would be away before they came.

I kept about my work, trembling all the time at heart, but said nothing, felt sure they had come, heard the dogs bark at times through the day, would not let my last turn of water be until sundown, but tremblingly went in the middle of the afternoon; then expecting to see swarthy figures spring, tiger-like, upon me from every thicket of oak bushes that grew along by my path; went out to milk at an early hour, when what should I see but an Indian bounding over the prairie on a white pony up to the house, almost with lightning speed. I went in and asked father and husband to come out on to the piazza if they could, and tell the Indian the reason of our being there. We recognized the Indian to be one of those who had been to our cabin at the Settlement. They tried to make him understand that we were sick, and had come to get

8

good cold water from "Indian spring." He went through with the same round of gestures many times, said, "Wau-shau-shas" (their name for Indians) "come!" pointing to the white top of our wigwam made signs that they would see it and come. He would put his hand against the house making signs that it was "Wau-shau-sha's;" then strike his hand and blow through it, making signs again that they would be angry, cut us all to pieces, and scatter us over the prairies. He delivered his ill omen, mounted his pony, and went dashing away as fast as he came, toward the dilapidated city of wigwams. For a moment we were all silent!—all thinking the same, —that we had had a timely warning, that this Indian was friendly to us, and had warned us of danger. Who should break the silence! who should propose what was to be done at this critical hour, when not one but myself could walk one-half mile! I knew I must be the one to act—the one to lead the way. I asked my husband what we should do—answering it in the same breath, that I knew what was to be done!—I must go to the Settlement and get men and teams, to come and take us away. He said nothing—I knew by his silence that he felt we were in danger and approved of my plan, but felt that it was dangerous for me to go alone, yet knew there was no other way. I equipped myself with my husband's long hickory cane, not for defence, but to assist me in my flight. I took leave of them all with as much calmness as I could summon, embracing my husband and darling children, perhaps for the last time—then pressing my Willie, my *baby boy*, once again to my heaving bosom, started off when the sun was only one-half hour above the horizon. I walked, run, or flew, not knowing which, feeling that speed was necessary, there being no twilight in this country, for when the sun goes down, darkness begins; and if I did not get in sight of the Settlement before it was dark, I might get lost on the broad prairie. Kept looking in every direction for the red men, expecting every moment they might appear in the way before me; but not all the four thousand would have hindered me from making an effort to save my family from the awful doom that loomed up before me; that of being massacred by the Indians.

I had often read of people's fleeing from the Indians, but now it was coming to me in all its frightful reality. I remembered in that anxious hour that I had heard it remarked that the Osages were very superstitious; they had been taught that they would displease the "Great Spirit" by being out nights. So I thought, "if they should not come upon them to-night, and I can get them away before they are out in the morning, I shall save them."

By sundown I had reached the cornfield, two miles; I hurried on to reach the top of the next prairie swell, where I should be in sight of Mr. Adams'; that being gained, and I not taken by the Indians, I kept my eye on the house and reached it just as it was getting so dark that a few minutes later no object could have been seen. I entered almost breath-

less, quickly told Mr. Adams our danger and what
I wanted. He, though weak with chills and fever,
started immediately for the Broadbents, one mile,
took the younger; then on two miles further to the
Stewarts, aroused them and with lanterns in hand
looked up the oxen on the prairie, put two pair before an open wagon, and at eleven at night he came
with a team, the younger Broadbent and Stewart to
accompany me back.

Meanwhile Mrs. Adams had striven to keep me
quiet and hopeful,—but the minutes lengthened into
months, the hours into years, and it seemed an age
of fear and trembling before we could get started.

It began to thunder and lighten. We knew a
storm was approaching;—but not all the artillery of
the heavens at once discharged, burning the earth
and air with lightning's fiery chains, could induce
me to wait another moment. Mrs. A. gave me a
thick woolen quilt to put around me, and we started, not either of the men having been to the Indian
house. The thunder roared, and our way was lit by
the flashing lightning;—but fortunately the shower
went round to the south, so we did not get very wet,
the quilt gave good protection to me. After we had
passed our cornfield, the men knew not which way
to go, and I feeling so confused, anxious, and bewildered, could not tell them. They changed the oxen,
putting the ones ahead that the elder Stewart had
driven up there when he went with his wife, and sat
quietly in the wagon and let them follow the instinct
they have, of going where they have been once.

The clouds cleared away, leaving the moon well up in the clear sky to light us on. The men then wanted I should look out and see if the oxen were really following their instinct, or taking us off another way on to the broad ocean of prairie. I could not recognize one of the scattering trees that we neared, but told them we should find such trees as we neared the looked-for house.

Pretty soon the men said they saw a light—then a house! My trembling heart leaped for joy—I knew they were safe—and if ever I returned grateful thanks to Heaven, it was at that hour. I met my family with embraces and rejoicings—it seemed as though years had separated us. Found they had been breathlessly anxious about me as I had been about them, for fear that I would be seized before I could reach the Settlement.

Sister L. was the only one able to sit up and keep a fire; she said my husband had sent her times without number out on to the piazza to listen for a sound like oxen and wagon approaching.

I gave the men each a blanket, and they were soon in quiet resting slumber. I laid me down, but no sleep or heaviness could close my eye-lids. I had been under too much mental suffering in the few past hours, to be easily quieted to sleep. I had experienced, as it were, an "ocean in a tear, a whirlwind in a sigh, an eternity in a moment;"—and the work of rescue was yet to be done.

As soon as a tinge of the approach of this holy

Sabbath morn painted the eastern sky, I was up,—
out to arouse my cow from her soft grassy bed,
where she lay as quietly as though all nature was
made for her, and compressed into the circle marked
by her bites around the oak bush to which she was
tied. She got leisurely up, stretching, breathing, and
chewing her cud, all unaware of the feverish hurry
of the one wanting to drain her large milk-bag of
its creamy contents, to make our already smoking
pudding relish for breakfast.

When our morning's repast was over, I began to
assist the men in arranging the two wagons so that
the sick ones could ride lying down on their beds.
At a very early hour this morn, we gladly bade
adieu to the old Indian house, with all its wild,
sepulchral, fear-of-massacre associations, and before
the Indian's whoop, their savage music made by
drumming on wolf-skin strained over hoops, or a
bark from their lean dogs had stirred the air, regret-
ting nothing that we left save the fountain of pure
cold water. When at the cornfield, found we had
sweet corn large enough to boil, and summer
squashes in abundance ; gave the men permission
to pick all they wished for, and laid in a good
store for ourselves, for we all felt the need of something fresh to eat.

On our arrival at our former cabin (the centre
Octagon) found that our neighbors had taken our
chamber floor to make improvements in their own
homes, and that the cattle had entered our cabin

(there being no door) and had stabled here just as
they pleased. The men went to work in good earnest with shovel and hoe; and when they had
cleared out the filth to the revealing of the stone-
paved floor, I began to use the broom. All this
time leaving the sick to keep their places in the
wagons.

Our kind neighbors went back two miles, after a
load of "*Punchuns*" that father had drawn from
the ruins of the Indian city to make him a shelter
to rest under and take his dinner when he was planting corn and making fence. They laid a floor part
way over in our loft, of the "*Punchuns*," on which
they placed my bed and some of our trunks.

Mother's bed is placed in its old corner, and sister
L.'s two boards laid on trunks in their former place.
Then the men went one mile over the river to a
good spring, and brought two pails of water for us
to drink.

So here we are again, in the " old mud house," as
the children call it, as comfortable as our kind neighbors, under surrounding circumstances, can make
us ; thankful, and even rejoicing with tears that we
have escaped from the Indians and all the horrors
that gather around their savage massacres ! And
again, let me fall down before the Divine Upholder,
and praise and thank Him that I have been helped
to remove the sick and pale ones from the place
where so many wild visions of death and struggle
floated in panoramic views before me ! We can bear

our trials better, here with the remnant of our company where all sympathize together, and are willing and anxious to do for each other's comfort and happiness.

CHAPTER IX.

" Ye good distressed! ye noble few!
  Who here unbending stand beneath life's pressure."

AUGUST 4TH.—The second man has returned that
was sent after the oxen; he brings in the report
that they were "taken up" at the Catholic Mission,
and put in a yard, but a little girl went to the yard
for something, left the bars down for a moment, and
they ran out and went bounding over the prairies
again in an easterly direction. They were sent for,
but they went so fast that they soon lost sight of
them. My husband has now hired the third man,
(a Mr. Morris, a young man who lives up the river,
and is well acquainted with the country out into
Missouri,) to go after them.

I have received a letter to-day, from my dear, good
friend, Mrs. V. She writes as follows:

"BIG BLUE CREEK, July 12, 1856.
Agreeable to my promise, I hasten to write you
at the first opportunity. We are eighteen miles
from Kansas City; have stopped here for a long

morning in the shade, this very hot day. Will reach
Kansas City to-morrow. I may not have an opportunity to write while there. We have got along
very well so far; have slept in the wagon every
night; have had but one storm. Traveling seems
to agree with Mr. V.; his health is improving daily;
he takes quite long walks. I have had a chill every
day since I left, though they grow lighter and lighter
every day. Yesterday it was a mere nothing; I
had no fever or sweating. Oh! my dear friends,
how do you all do now? where are you? yet all sick
in that strange land, that malarious place, so far from
all dear friends? Oh! how I wish you could all be
restored, in the twinkling of an eye, to a good home.
I am here among folks.

Why must friends be so endeared? why must they
meet only to part, perhaps forever, in this world?

I will write more, if I get time before Mr. W.
returns. If I should not, I bid you all an affectionate adieu.

JULY 13, P. M.—We are now within two miles of
Kansas City, which we "made" about noon, and
where we shall stay until to-morrow morning. We
are quite well; the weather is very hot and the
roads are very dusty. There is said to be no disturb-
ance in this region now. We have seen no border
ruffians passing through Westport; all seemed as
quiet and orderly as any Eastern city. O! my dear
friends, you cannot think how happy we are, to have
this place passed in safety, the most difficult and

dangerous part of our journey. We are now stopping at McGee's. Did I not take a last farewell gaze at the spot of our memorable first camping out? I assure you I did. O! my experience in Kansas; may I never pass through another such again! How thankful I am, a way has been opened at last for me to get out of it! When shall I hear that you are all safely removed from that place, to a happy home in a community such as your hearts desire.

Adieu; and may this find you all well and happy, is the prayer of   E. V.

Good, dear friend; how little you know or imagine what we have experienced in the last month! while you have been flying from savageism to civilization and enlightenment, and to a home where stand open arms and warm hearts to welcome and receive you, and a bountiful store to supply all your necessities.

But alas! alas! alas! for us.

> "*My friends*, do they now and then send
>   A wish or a thought after me?
> *   *   *   *   *   *   *   *
> "When I think of my own native land,
>   In a moment I seem to be there;
>   But alas! recollection at hand
>   Soon hurries me back to despair."

AUGUST 5TH.—Another most terrific thunder-storm

broke, last night, peal after peal, over head in deafening, crushing sound; and the lightning's glare seemed burning the heavens from pole to pole! the torrents of rain came right through the warped "shakes" on the roof; the wind was blowing—the mud, from the logs, and water, were flying in every direction through our cabin. I made every effort to keep my sick ones dry, but my husband, children, and myself, being in the loft, got completely drenched —and my husband and children had their chills in the midst of the storm. We kept our beds until a late hour this morning, as wet as they were, they being the most comfortable place, while the sun was drying up the water around.

Mr. Broadbent came this forenoon, went to the spring over the river again for water, making a walk of four miles from his tent to get two pails of water for us.

I bring water from the creek, where it stands just in the deep places, and they have to be dug out for that. This water will do to cook with and for washing.

The Indians pass every day in long files, on ponies and on foot, going to Cofuchigue " to swap," as they say, their dried buffalo meat, tallow and robes, for coffee, sugar, tobacco and whisky. Their ponies of burden are so heavily loaded that the juveniles who ride them have their limbs horizontally extended, instead of hanging down. Their many long-eared, grizzly-gray, gaunt-looking dogs, bring up the rear.

How they can keep alive such a drove of dogs after their hunt is over, and keep them in going order, is truly a problem not for me to solve. They look like so many hungry hyenas; I should think they would swallow both horse and rider, and "lick their chops for more." Their buffalo meat is relished by some. It seems to be clean, and sweet; it is cured without salt, by being cut into strips, braided, the braids woven into a web, with strings of bark, and dried in smoke; can be bought by the yard, half or fourth, just as one desires or their appetite craves.

Some of the squaws have been here to-day ; wanted to "swap" some of their dried buffalo meat for some pumpkins we had in our cabin. I gave them the pumpkins, and they handed back some dried meat. Father and the children relish it. Willie says, "please mamma, give Willie some dried buffalo meat." We have so little change in our diet, that almost anything is relished. We have plenty of green corn and squashes, but I am afraid to let the sick satisfy their appetites, which have become craving, as they always do, after having the chills for a while. I can persuade my *little* children to lay the cob by for a little, with the corn half eaten off; but it is a difficult matter to persuade children whose heads are gray with age, for "they know, they guess, when they have eaten enough, and when they are hungry."

AUGUST 7TH.—The symptoms of the sick are more

favorable; some are missing their chills for a day or two, others for a day. I wish I could hope that they might be all well in a few days.

Have been to Mr. V'.s cornfield, near by, for corn; there are plenty of peas, beans and cucumbers there, and soon will be any quantity of large ripe water-melons and muskmelons. Mrs. V'.s morning-glories are running all over the cornstalks, and must present a beautiful array of flowers at the early dawn of these clear, dewy mornings, lavishing their delicate odor on the air. The tomatoes that she planted with her own hands, are large and rank in growth, bending to the ground with their load of large, nice red tomatoes.

Our last meal being over for to-day, and milking done, will spend a little time now, just as the ground is being dampened with dew, to cut a pile of it for my calf, which is going through the process of wean-ing, living entirely on grass. I suppose it thinks it is hard fare to be shut up in a little pen of poles here in front of the cabin, and have nothing but grass and dish-water. I think calfie eats a big stock of grass in twenty-four hours, and all I am obliged to cut with an Indian knife.

AUGUST 10TH.—My husband awoke me this morn-ing, by saying, "Why, Miriam, what is the matter? you seem almost convulsed with grief." As soon as I could speak, I said, "I have just been dreaming that our Willie boy was taken sick with a disease of the bowels, and that he died; dreamed we were in a large and beautiful town, where there were many trees, and a great many people, and that the people were extremely kind; that we rode in black carriages to the place of burial, which was almost in a lonely, shady wood, and that the men were just lowering our darling's coffin down into the grave, when you awoke me. Do you wonder that I was weeping? And it has impressed me so that I am still trembling."

"Well, now, my dear," said my husband, "do not give yourself any unnecessary trouble about your dream; you know you are my 'dreamer,' but not all of your dreams come to pass."

"Don't you remember," said I, "that Joseph was sarcastically called the 'dreamer,' by his brethren; and do you not think that the same power that impressed Joseph in his dreams could impress me? Oh! I hope my dream will not come to pass, and I know it cannot in all its picturings, because we do not expect ever to go away from this place now."

A large number of Indians have been around our fire to-day, asking me to light their pipes for them, which I reluctantly did. They called for water; my husband told them that his "squaw" was sick, pointing to me, and that they must go to the creek, pointing that way. So they were soon off with themselves, in their wild glee, with their drums, horns, ponies and dogs.

I spread blankets on the "punchuns" out by the side of the cabin, these hot afternoons, minding to get the shady side, for the invalids to go and lie on, to take the cool breeze; and sometimes I made a chair for them, by turning the wash-tub bottom side up, putting the end board of the wagon for the back, and spreading an Indian blanket thereon.

Mr. Adams, and his wife and child have got the chills, and the two young men are still sick.

Mr. Stewart's people are sick likewise, though they thought they had worn the disease all out in Illinois.

AUGUST 11TH.—My husband has been anxious to see Mr. Clubb at his present abiding place, up on Stony Creek, ten miles from here, to see if he would refund any of the money that he put into his hands. So to-day, our good neighbor, Mr. Hobbs, was kind enough to take us there. I made the wagon as bed-like as I could with blankets and pillows, so that my husband could ride lying down, also my Willie, who wanted to go with us. Our good neighbor, Mr. Hobbs, took us safely over high prairies, through deep ravines, past fine cornfields, where some settlers were getting a good start, through Stony Creek, where all the water was dried up, and along up by its dry bed, until we arrived at the little cabin, where we found our Secretary confined to his bed with fever. We rested and took some dinner that Mrs. Clubb cooked by a fire some rods from the cabin, to prevent the smoke from entering it to annoy the sick. Mr. Clubb had no money to refund, but let us have some corn starch, farina, a few dates, and a little pearled barley.

A shower came up while we were coming home, but our good, thick wagon top and blankets kept us from getting wet. My husband missed his chill to-day, and feels better for the ride; thinks it would cure him to travel.

It is rumored that H. S. Clubb has resorted to his present abode, that he may make his way quietly out of the Territory. We can take advantage of no law to regain our money paid to him for the company.

AUGUST 14TH.—We have had a drizzling rain for two or three days, which is very unusual for this season of the year in this country. It has been very bad for the sick, so damp inside without a fire. I have had a wet time going after my cow, off on the prairie, and bringing water through the tall wet grass. I put on my husband's boots, and tuck my calico pants into the tops, but then the grass is a great deal higher than my boots, so that I get wet to my waist, as though I had walked in the river. The cow is getting to be very unmanageable since I weaned her calf. Sometimes when I have been more than a mile after her, and have driven her almost to our cabin, she will turn and bound off over the prairie like a deer. I then am obliged to let her go, and we do without milk, for I might go miles after her and not get her. There have been two days that I could not get her; then we ate our gruel with just a little salt. When I succeed in getting her nights now, I tie her up to the ends of the logs at the corner of our cabin, but then the oxen come and hook her, so that I am obliged to get up many times in the night to drive them away.

I must get Mr. Hobbs to picket her; then I shall have to bring water for her, but that will be much easier than to chase after her as I have done.

This day is now at its close, with its toils and their recordings. I have looked after all the wants as far as I have the means. I am weary, very weary; my clothes are damp and uncomfortable. I could hope for brighter days to dawn upon us, but our sky is clouded; a little light now and then glimmers through the darkness, but soon again the clouds close over, and all is dark. Will Heaven grant to us a dawning?

AUGUST 16TH.—For days my husband has been trying to persuade father to leave the Territory, telling him that we can go out into Missouri, where we shall be in the world, among people, and where, if we should be sick until late in the Fall or Winter, and need the kindness of people, we should be where there were people to bestow that kindness. But it is all in vain to talk to him; he cannot be moved one inch from his position; he says we may go, but that he shall stay and sell the land that has been taken up in the family; that as he is getting so much better now he will soon be able to build a fireplace in the cabin, make a door and put in windows, and then get his goods in from Kansas City.

My husband thinks now, that if another opportunity presents, he shall improve it and leave the Territory. Has been trying to get mother to say that she will go too, leaving sister L. to stay with father until he shall have sold the land—then come to us wherever we shall be. Father is very sure that he will realize quite a sum from the nearly 1000 acres of land held in our family, the timber being so valuable.

Our good neighbor, Broadbent, came with his oxen to-day, put them before our wagon, and all of us but mother and sister L. took a ride to our cornfield. The rows of corn are very straight and tall, and the ripe golden ears look rich in the sunlight; but the Indians have ridden their ponies through a part of it, and broken some of it down; they are picking it and will soon carry off and destroy the whole six acres. They are taking the pumpkins; and of father's large patch of big musk and watermelons, that he was going to feast on, not even one little green one remains.

The settlers are obliged to watch their cornfields now, in order to save their corn from these thieving Indians; so that every man is busy watching for himself. Neither father nor my husband is well enough to walk to the cornfield at morning dawn and watch until nightfall, to save their six acres, which would yield at least fifty bushels of corn per acre. It seems hard and cruel, after all of their labor and toil, to have it sacrificed to these wild, idle, and improvident savages.

Mr. Broadbent said, two or three days ago a posse of Indians came to their tent, pretending to want to buy melons, and while they were bargaining for them, another posse, understanding the game, stripped the vines and made off with the melons. Such is their sly intriguing nature; it makes me shudder with fear to have them stand around our cabin, finishing up their arrows, and looking so sharply at us when they think we don't know it.

Mr. Morris has returned without our oxen, though he heard of them out in Missouri; he thinks some of the half-breed Indians have taken them. It is the law of the country that stray oxen shall be taken up and yarded such a length of time, to give the owner a chance to find them ; and if that law had been adhered to, our oxen might have been saved. My husband paid $75 last Spring for them, and now has paid $30 more to have them hunted up, and all is gone! The wagon will be of no use now without oxen.

SUNDAY, AUGUST 17TH.—I was up this morning as soon as yonder sun sent his bright rays aslant the broad fields of grass, peering in between the logs of our cabin, tinging the pale cheek, for the moment, with the flush of health, dissipating the dew drops, and ascending majestically on up into the clear blue dome of heaven, bringing in a most resplendent day. Though the heart be sad, and the limbs have not been rested through the night from toil, the soul must go out in silent adoration and praise to the Former of yon bright orb, which makes the day and night, sending forth his genial rays to inspire hope, and light up the path of the " pilgrim stranger."

The sick ones are certainly getting better. Sister L. and Mema went with me to-day when I went for water; while I was down in the bottom land dipping water from the standing pools, they busied themselves gathering flowers. The yellow sensitive plant is all in bloom; it grows something like a brake, with bright yellow flowers growing all along on the under side of the stalk; its seeds are enclosed in pods like peas. The hop vines, supported by saplings, are loaded with full-grown hops; and clustering all in among the green leaves of the grape-vine, is its rich fruit yet green. The prairies are still decked with flowers that come peeping up above the tall grass, as if asking for homage. But my time is precious.

Our good neighbors keep us well supplied with wild red plums; they are very sweet and delicious, as are the strawberry tomatoes which are indigenous to the soil. The prairie hens are still flapping their wings in the dry tree in the gulch below our cabin. The white crow, with the same caw as the black, is flying through the clear air up against the blue sky;

and was it not for the caw, would think it as pure as its color, a bird just sent out from angel bowers. There are many songsters enlivening the woodlands to-day; but none dare approach our cabin save the chubby quail, who is calling for "*wheat, wheat.*"

A letter has come over the long distance from our dear friend Mrs. V. She writes as follows:

PLAINFIELD, WIS., July 22, 1856.

MY DEAR FRIENDS: Arrived at home safely, and in much better health than when I left you. Arrived here at home just in two weeks from the time that we left the Neosho. Had a very pleasant journey. How happy I was, my dear friends, to find my father's family all well and happy, and O! how prosperous. They certainly have been signally blest. The crops are most abundant; corn looks better than in Missouri. This is a beautiful country; it never looked so good to me before. I must tell you, Mr. Colt, that father says, and all the neighbors too, that there are thousands of acres of land to be taken in this vicinity, and any amount of wheat harvesting to be had on shares—no trouble. Father says there will be some place to stay in for the first few weeks. O, well, there is no *trouble*, no *difficulty* in the least; my parents and all the neighbors invite you to come; they will certainly insure you all profitable employment. Come, now! School teachers are in great demand, both in the academies and district schools, around here. Oh! do come! The air is so pure and bracing—how can you be sick? It seems to infuse life and vigor immediately into me. Oh! if you would only come, you could live with us a while. Mr. V. left me in Chicago for his home. His health was very much better than when he left your settlement. Be sure to write immediately on the receipt of this. I must say again, oh! how I wish you would come! Our people here all want to see you; you certainly will not regret making a home here. How I hope you will come. That this may find you all well, is the sincere wish and prayer of your friend, E. V.

Dear, good friend. I could wish we were all transferred to your pleasant Wisconsin home; but my heart has so long vibrated between hope and fear, that to get away from this place seems almost an impossibility. I ask my husband many times a day if he thinks we shall ever get away. He says, "I am determined to go now, let father do as he will. I have written to St. Louis, to have the forwarders retain our goods there, if they have not already been sent to Kansas City."

August 19th.—Have been saving a little water every day now, for some days, to get enough to wash with, or make a pretension. Truly we are in a land where there is neither soap nor water; so how can we keep clean? What would my mother say, if she should see the color of what we call our white clothes?

I think she would say, as one Bohemian said to another, when asked, "Why, is not my shirt clean?" "Well, yes—it's clean for brown—but it's awful dirty for white." So it is with our white clothes, they are "awful dirty for white."

We laid off our night clothes when we came into the Territory, and have slept without them, (except when we needed them very much to shelter us from the musquetoes,) because I could not bear to have them take on the brown color, which they must necessarily for the want of soap and water.

Have taken the chinking out from between the logs, to let the wind blow freely through our loft, so now we can sleep some when the wind blows hard enough in one side to blow the musquetoes out the other. Another improvement is, that the cow is picketed, so I don't have to chase after her—but it is no improvement to my arms, which feel as though the bones were drawn from their sockets now, bringing water for the cow to drink. Willie is afraid when I go for water, that the Indians will carry off his mamma; so, when he feels well enough, he will stand out by the side ·of our cabin and look after me; when I go down into the bottom lands I am out of sight; when I come up again on to the prairie, I can still see his little yellow head by the side of the cabin; he thinks I am safe when he can see me. Darling boy! his golden locks are more than a mine of gold to his mother.

AUGUST 24TH.—We have been intending to start for Kansas City, the twenty-sixth of this month. Our trunks are packed and labeled, and every preparation made that circumstances will admit of for our journey. Have put the clothes that we shall need when we take the steamer into one trunk to have them handy. Have made a little sack of hard water crackers, for my husband says he shall not be well enough to eat the rich food they have on board the steamers. But our way is hedged up again; the younger Broadbent was to take us, but he and his brother are both sick, unable even to get out of their tent, and no one to take care of them only as a well one goes in. Yesterday, after my usual round at home, I walked there, one mile, taking them some milk, brought water, and cooked victuals for them. Mr. Adams came here this morning; said he had no wood to make a fire, and that they all went without supper last night; he looked pale and weak; I gave him some of our farina gruel with bread-cakes crumbed into it; then made the gruel camp-pail full putting in a good quantity of milk, for him to take home, with the rest of my bread-cakes.

I soon followed him, taking along some milk, then went for water for them. Mr. Adams said, " Mrs. Colt, I never could have got home without the strength that that gruel gave me." Mr. Stewart has been and chopped some wood for them, and has also been here and brought some fine ripe muskmelons. Their melon patch is so near their cabin that the Indians have not yet stolen them.

The eighth of September the Indians meet at the Indian Agent's, to receive their annuities from government; then the damages done to the white settlers is taken out, and the damage paid. Father says he shall have the damage done to the cornfield prized, go and present it and get pay. They have not disturbed the Voorhees cornfield, only taken all the melons.

The sick ones are a good deal better; they have been taking some patent medicine—though we do not think much of such medicine, still we have been induced to try it by our good friends, the Stewarts; they had been in the habit of taking it in Illinois, and recommend it highly.

AUGUST 25TH.—This morning father and my husband started off, to go nine miles below here, to deliver the wagon, which had been sold, and receive payment. They fastened an old sled behind the wagon, on which to ride back. It is not such bad sledding in this country in August, as one would suppose; the prairie grass is very wiry, and a sled passes over it without any grinding; the sled shoes going through the process of sharpening all the time. I have been very anxious all day about them, fearing they would get sick, but they have returned safely; my husband is very tired—father has stood it well.

Arrangements have been made with Mr. Morris to take us out of the Territory. We leave on the morning of the 28th. We hear of late, that serious trouble has commenced again, between the Border Ruffians and the Free State settlers, extending from Kansas City and Westport, down south as far as Fort Scott, and that it will not be safe to pass through either of the above named places. We intend to pass out of the Territory south of Fort Scott, into Southern Missouri, and from there strike the Missouri river at the nearest point.

AUGUST 28TH.—This morning early found me at my post, bringing water through the dewy grass for ourselves, and the picketed cow. Our simple meal being over, my children were dressed as clean as I could have them, and ready for journeying,—myself arrayed in a clean Bloomer,—our provisions put into the dinner pail,—and we sat waiting for our teamster to come with oxen and wagon.

We have waited all day—have looked and looked away in the clear sun-light, to see the white-topped wagon come over the green prairies, but no wagon has come! It is almost sundown now, and our wonderings and questions have not been answered, as to the reason of detainment. The children have been very impatient; I have walked out with them, gathered flowers, and have tried to divert them, when I have been more disappointed than they could possibly be. My husband has kept very quiet, so as to quiet his wife and children. We must go to our loft again, without knowing the reason of our disappointment.

AUGUST 30TH.—Mr. Morris sent us word to-day, that he will not be able to take us out of the Territory. He intends leaving with his family, in company with another, on account of the northern troubles.

Father has just returned from the cornfield, with a sled-load of pumpkins that the Indians had not tugged away; he has piled them up in one corner of the cabin; says he is going to live on pumpkin-pies after we go away. We know of no way now to get out of the Territory.

SUNDAY, AUG. 31ST.—A bright, bright day! All nature is quiet; a silent adoration from prairie, wood, and dell, seems to be borne away on the bright sun light, to Him who holds all nature in the "hollow of his hand;" and shall we mortals withhold our praise? No! though we worship in the shade of disappointment, our Author demands an offering.

My husband, though no dreamer, has just been relating to me the dream he dreamt last night. He said, "I dreamt that we left this place, and travelled a very long distance, until we came to a large river; then we stood on the bank considering how we were to get across it. Finally, we concluded to ford it; so you took one child and I the other, and soon came out on the other side. There we found a beautiful country—all kinds of fruit were growing spontaneously, and in abundance—every want was satisfied, and we were happy."

When we were expecting to leave, my husband

gave the cow and calf to sister L.; told her that they were well worth forty dollars, and that the worth of them would take her out of the Territory any time she wished to leave. His planes, augers, saws, and all such tools, he has given to father; has divided the remainder of the money, keeping for ourselves just what, with the cheapest fare, would take us to some point on the other side of the Mississippi, either to Wisconsin or to New York.

There is a spike of splendid scarlet flowers that has been in blossom for some time, and is still blossoming at the top. If I leave this place, I intend to pick it the last time I go for water, as it is just beside my path, near the pool, and press it in my portfolio, as a memento of some of my toils.

SEPT. 1ST.—This morning Mr. Wheeler came in, and gave my husband an invitation to ride to Mr. Stewart's on their pony; said he could walk back; thought he was strong enough. I followed them, to see how they were going to get along, they both being weak, across the creek into the little wood beyond, where they sat down on the grass just at the edge of the prairie, to talk over our late disappointment. When they went on I came back to our cabin.

Very soon Mr. Blackburn came in and asked if we were intending to leave the Territory. I told him we had made up our minds that there would probably be no more opportunities for getting away.

He said that Mr. Henly was going out into Missouri
in a day or two, with an empty wagon, after provisions.

I immediately followed on to Mr. Stewart's, and
related what Mr. B. had said. My husband told
me to go on to Mr. Henly's, and see what he would
ask to take us and Mr. Wheeler out into Missouri.
I started off with a bound, over the prairie, through
the grass as high as my head, on an Indian trail,
passing a ledge of rocks, where was a den of rattlesnakes, without looking to see whether snake-dom
was out sunning itself or not—just stooping to pluck
a fine ripe prickly pear at my feet—eating the delicious strawberry-flavored fruit as I hastened along,
putting the seeds into my pocket. Found Mr. Henly tinkering his wagon, to get it in order for his
journey. The sum was agreed upon, that would
recompense him for taking us out to Mt. Vernon,
Lawrence county, Missouri. I asked him when he
thought he should be ready to go? He said, "If
my wife can get my clothes finished, I will start to-
morrow morning, in company with Morris and Wil-
bern." I told Mrs. Henly that I would sit down
and sew two hours; that I thought I could then get
back in season for my night chores. In two hours'
hard sewing, by us both, the needed garments were
finished. I was then feasted on fine, ripe, delicious
water-melon, such as I never had tasted in northern
land. Mr. Henly had loads and loads of them growing in his cornfield like pumpkins, and so near his

cabin that the Indians had not dared to meddle with them. I then started with my umbrella and a watermelon as large as a pumpkin, on my three miles walk.

When out on the prairie, up galloped an Indian on his pony with his saluting "hi!" He took out his large knife from his belt, and made signs for my melon; I handed it to him (for I dared not do otherwise); he took it, cut it, and gave back two-thirds, which was more than I expected, nodded his thanks, and went on.

I lost some of my melon, but it lightened my load. Reached Mr. Stewart's; told my husband I had made arrangements to start in the morning, and that Mr. Wheeler could go too.

We started for our place of abode, but my husband found that he was too weak to walk; told me to go and get everything ready for our start in the morning, and he would go back and ride down in the morning when the team came along. So here I am again—have feasted the remaining ones on the big melon, and been the usual round of night chores —find myself tired and my arms lame from lugging the melon.

CHAPTER X.

OUR JOURNEY FROM THE NEOSHO, ETC.

"And the first clouds and mountains seem the last :
But, those attain'd, we tremble to survey
The growing labors of the lengthen'd way ;
Th' increasing prospect tires our wand'ring eyes ;
Hills peep o'er hills, and Alps on Alps arise."

SEPTEMBER 2D.—I was up this morning at early
dawn, cooking for our journey, and bringing water
to fill all empty vessels, to make the task lighter
through the day for sister L. and father, who was
having a slight chill. Made myself and children
ready again—got our good neighbor, Mr. Hobbs, to
strap our trunks and take our bed of prairie grass
from the loft, to be ready to place in the wagon, so
that my husband and children can lie on it to ride
through the days, and for us to sleep on nights. I
then went for my last turn of water, and to pick my
spike of flowers ; bade farewell to all the windings
of my path to the water, and to the trees, vines,
grass, and flowers, which had seemed to bow in silent
sympathy at my sad lamentations, and listened to
the breathings of my prayer—to these unspoken

friends I bade a *last* adieu. Soon the wagon was seen coming towards the creek, and the other two moving in a straight line on the prairie, with which we were soon to fall in rear. Our trunks were placed in the back end of the wagon, where were stowed a fine lot of watermelons; our bed in front, and our dinner pail so as to have it handy. Children were in a hurry to ride, and teamster to get up with the other wagons. I bade farewell to father, mother and sister L. with a sad heart, and placed my children and self into the wagon; my husband still lingered; it was a time of heart-trial to him to leave his own father, mother, and sister in this wild land, when he had made such earnest appeals to them to leave. Father's tenacious will must bind his wife and daughter.

We start out upon the world again. Many a dark shade has passed over us since last Spring. We move up along on to the high prairie; I keep my eye on the log cabin we have left; could leave the cabin without a sigh, but for those left there must breathe many. We make a little descent, it shuts the whole view from my eyes forever!

Now I will take a look at the picture before me: here are my husband and children, very weak; we move along at a very slow pace; hundreds of miles are before us, and know not where we shall find a resting place. I must take the burden! How are we to reach the summit of the mountain that rises before us? May Heaven grant strength and courage!

10

Wé soon fall in rear of the other wagons, presenting quite the appearance of a caravan; while treading along behind are mules, oxen, cows and calves. We move on through the tall grass over the Indian lands. The Indians are riding about on their ponies, all at ease, with the fleetness of deer. We pass Godfrey's, nine miles; stop to bait the oxen; we have passed Big Creek, where my husband was intending to take claims; it was high, and a beautiful prospect presented itself to the eye; we go on down on to lower prairie; six miles more, arrive at Canveal's, (a Frenchman,) and to a camping-ground all in among the wild sunflowers. We have taken our suppers; it is raining, and the dusky shades of night are coming on. My husband has gone to "Monsieur" Canveal's, to see if he can get lodgings for the night. I and my children will sleep in the wagon, Mr. Wheeler and Henly under it; I see that they are beginning to retire in the other two wagons, and under them; my head is aching hard. I *over-done* this morning, bringing water, and that with the excitement of leaving, has caused it. May Heaven protect, to-night, the sick, anxious, and weary travelers.

SEPTEMBER 3D.—Cooked breakfast by camp-fire. My husband took his with "Monsieur" Canveal; had a pleasant time with him; found him to be formerly from Montreal, our once happy home; but said the dogs liked to have eaten him up before he could get to the house last night. It seems necessary to keep a score of dogs in this country; I suppose it is for protection. My husband's good host would not allow him to depart without first shooting down chanticleer for him to take along for his dinner; so when a fire was kindled in a pleasant wood to cook dinner by, I had the fowl disrobed of feathers and skin, all to one pull by a strong man's hand, and soon it was boiling in a kettle set on to the fire. When tender, it was seasoned with nothing but salt, leaving in a good quantity of broth; the kettle was then placed on a log, my husband, Mr. Wheeler, my children and self, composing my family, got around it, with bread in hand, and soon the kettle was empty. It was quite a change in diet for us.

We passed the Catholic Mission this afternoon. It is said to be the most flourishing school in the Territory. It was founded in 1847. Rev. John Schoenmaker has discharged the duties of Superior in an efficient manner since the commencement, assisted by two Jesuit clergymen and lay teachers. The little Indian boys were out as we passed, in high glee.

We find ourselves, to-night, on Hickory Creek. But little timber skirts its borders; clumps of bushes scattered along, make a pleasing variety. Have cooked some rice and made some tea for our supper. Our company all feel full of glee; they are picketing their mules and cows, and milking, to have milk for their coffee. My husband tries to be cheerful as he sits by the camp-fire, with his Indian blanket around him. My head aches; I have ridden lying down all day,—and my heart is sad, very sad.

SEPTEMBER 4TH.—Our journeying to-day has been over fine prairies, and through woodlands that just skirted the small streams; but they were complete bowers of vines; all over head, on the trees, were grape vines, bending with the weight of fruit, and all over the ground and shrubs, smaller vines, not so aspiring, and of many kinds, were woven into one complete mat; they were charmingly beautiful, and the deep shade and rich perfume, was cooling and refreshing upon a hot day like this.

One of Henly's oxen has been lame to-day, which has kept us moving at a slow rate. The wagons are drawn up in the camping form, here on Cow Creek, on the borders of the Cherokee Indian lands, in Missouri. We are now fairly out of Kansas. It is really amusing to look on and see with what ease and home-like feeling, these Southern "Squatter Sovereigns" adapt themselves to an out-door life. They have their cooking utensils, bacon, corn meal, and coffee, all stored in a little addition on the back end of their wagons; and as soon as a halting is made, at noon or night, the fire is struck up, out comes the tea-kettle, and over the fire it goes, or rather is placed *on* the fire; the tray and corn meal come next, and the bread is soon baking in the

Dutch oven; then the bacon is put to frying in the spider,—and soon the men, women and children are sitting around on the grass, partaking of the quickly-made meal, with a keen relish.   They sometimes put corn bread, bacon and coffee, all into one dish, and call it "bucket soup."   The water is very bad here; a green scum covers the top of it; have made tea of it, and cooked some rice in it; my husband and Mr. Wheeler drank the tea, and my darling children are so thirsty they must drink this water, that is so full of disease.   I could not bear to taste of the rice; have eaten one of the hard water crackers for my supper, and drank no tea or water.   A settler, a mile above, attracted by our camp-fire, has come down to see who we are, and is relating all the bloody war news of Northern Kansas.   It is misty and cool to-night; have hung a blanket up at the front end of the wagon to keep out the damp air and the musquetoes.   My children are in bed for the night, and so is their papa.   I must make a few more notes in my diary, with my candle standing on our provision pail.   I could feel glad to-night, to think that we are out of Kansas, were it not for those that are still in that land, and that I must look at the "lengthened way" before us.   I often amuse and quiet my children, by telling them of the many good things they shall have when they get home—but where is our home?

> "If ceaseless, thus, the fowls of Heaven He feeds;
> If o'er the fields such lucid robes He spreads;
> Will He not care for you, ye faithless, say?
> Is *He unwise?* or are ye less than they?"

SEPTEMBER 5TH.—We campers were up with the coming in of morning,—our camp-fire supplied with coal, which crops out all along on Cow Creek. After our breakfasting, all of us women and girls stood around the fire, in the misty air, just before taking to our wagons, when one of the women said to me:

"Do you mop?"

I said, "what?"

"Do you mop?"

"Why," said I, "what do you mean?"

She said, "do you mop your teeth with snuff? most of the Southern ladies do," she taking me to be a Southern lady. I then noticed that she was "mopping" her teeth with a little swab, first dipped into her snuff box. So I learned what she meant by asking me if I "mopped." I then remembered of reading of such a practice among Southern ladies.

We have passed cornfields, orchards and gardens to-day; have traveled in a road that was fenced off. It seemed so natural, yet so strange, to see so many precursors of civilization. We have also passed a grocery, and our teamster took occasion to have his tin bottle filled with "fire-water," as the Indians call whisky, and has kept sipping it since. He has promised us all day that he would take us to a house to stay to-night, but when we came on to the camp-ground, just before sundown, refused to take us one-fourth of a mile further, to a house. My husband told him he was not using us right, and as he agreed; upon which he went into a frenzy of rage, and dealt out oaths like any intoxicated man. It was necessary for me to go somewhere to buy some-thing for our suppers; so I left the children with Mr. Wheeler, and started off with my husband for the nearest house. Found a good, kind family, by the name of Seeker, who invited us to stay in their house. The good people were getting supper. I could hardly realize that I was gazing upon the home comforts of chairs, tables, good beds, upon bedsteads, and a plenty of good food cooked as though there was a bounteous store of provisions. The good old lady was just taking a loaf of wheat bread, from a Dutch oven, of the capacity of half a bushel; I think I must have looked at it with eagerness, for it was the largest loaf of bread that I ever saw; its whiteness and fresh flavor, being just out of the ov-en, and its mammoth size, were enough to recom-mend it to my palate, and I thought it would to the palates of my children, who would be so pleased with some white bread. I was invited to take sup-per, but declined, feeling thankful that my husband was going to fare so well through the night; took some bread and milk and hurried along, (just stop-ping to pick a fine cluster of blossoms from a honey-suckle that had interwoven with a grape on a small tree by the side of the road,) back to the wagon just at dark; I found my children sitting on the wagon tongue; I offered Mema some of the rich orange-colored flowers of a finger's length, but she did not want any; I gave them to Willie; he said. "Mamma, Mema cried when you was gone; Willie didn't cry." I then served Mr. Wheeler, my children and self, with bread and milk, all sitting on the wagon tongue. The other two families have been through their round of baking, frying, and making coffee, with the addition of stewing apples, which they took when we passed the orchard.

It begins to rain hard; Henly is putting the quilts over the top of the wagon, which he brought for that purpose; keeps swearing, to relieve his sur-charged system, I suppose, and reaching his hand in for more pins, to pin the quilts on to the wagon top. Myself and children have the whole of the inside of the wagon to-night. Mr. Wheeler and our intoxi-cated teamster have taken to their berth under the wagon. It is raining like a shower.

SEPTEMBER 6TH.—It rains hard this morning; all of us travellers are obliged to huddle in here at good Mrs. Seeker's, to cook our breakfast. My husband says he rested well last night on the soft bed, and has partaken of a good breakfast this morning. My Willie is in a chill; I have laid him *on to a bed*. The rain subsides—the clouds clear away, the wag-ons are ready, and the teamsters say, "come le'ts be off!" I take my Willie from the good bed, and lay him on our bed in the wagon; we are on the move again; Henly is full of invective. Two o'clock; the two families have got the loan of a little vacant house here by the roadside, and they propose stopping the rest of the day and night, to cook and rest; our driver stops too; we had rather go on.

Our dinner over, Henly, under the influence of liquor, comes up to our wagon, takes out his large knife, begins to whet it on the wheel, and says, "I am a Border Ruffian! now, your blood or your money!" It was useless for my husband to say anything to appease his wrath, for he seemed to be burning with fury against him. He spoke low to me, saying, "you try to quiet him." I said, "I think he thinks that perhaps he wont get his pay for bringing us out, and I had better take the portmonnaie and pay him our fare." I paid him and spoke kindly to him, for I could see that a spark would explode him,—then we might look out for our blood. The above scare so overcame my husband that he began to have a chill. I went a little way back with him to a house, where they gave him permission to spread his blanket down on the floor, and stay until morning, where he would be out of hearing of the drunken oaths of our ruffian driver. I said to myself, "I must go back, and if there are any battles to be fought, must put on manly bravery and fight them, and stay with my precious children, who dare not stir out of the wagon." Bought some provisions, and have been cooking in the house with the other famili**.

Henley declares that he wont take us another mile, but will put our trunks out here by the side of the road. He has had his bottle filled again, and is treating all the negroes, I guess, on the plantation. Fearing him, I have been and left our money and gold watch with my husband. Am here in the wagon to comfort my children. It is growing dark; can see his disgustful figure gliding here and there, with the negroes, among the clumps of bushes. May an Arm, stronger and higher than mine, be over and around us to-night.

SEPTEMBER 7TH.—It was late last night before our drunken driver got quiet. He came to the wagon where I and my children were trying to rest, and began insulting me with his vile words and oaths; I used my greatest effort to appear quiet, and talk calmly, when my heart was bounding with fear, and filled with "holy indignation," and some I guess that was not so holy. He finally went off, cursing me at a great rate, to an old house where Mr. Wheeler had found a lodging place on a pile of flax. This morning his liquor had somewhat evaporated, and our kind fellow-travelers persuaded him to take us ten miles further, where we should be on the road to Boonville, but not so far as I had paid him for, into thirty miles. I went to the house where my husband was; told him Henly was going to take us on a few miles, and that he must get up. The lady of the house made him a cup of coffee and a piece of toast. We bade them good morning, thanking the lady for her kindness, and soon were on our way. Mr. Wheeler, self and children, took our breakfast on the way, in the wagon.

Arrived here in Carthage, Jasper county, about three o'clock this afternoon; found a room here in the house of a Mr. Wells, whose family seem very kind. Are glad to let our drunken ruffian teamster go along without going any further with him. Have had some supper, made our bed upon the floor, and feel that we can rest.

SEPTEMBER 8TH.—It seems good and strange to be in the world again : I can look out, see roads, houses, streets, carriages, and people going this way and that way. It is a long time since I have looked upon such a picture as this. This pleasant little town is the county seat; the court house is just across the green, and a public well is there, where I should think all the folks of the town go for water.

My husband and children are sick to-day with the chills again. Mr. Wheeler is very weak. Mrs. Wells has a little child sick with the dysentery. I feel under obligation to help her what I can, besides taking care of our own sick ones, she is so very kind.

SEPTEMBER 12TH.—Yesterday I gave medicine to stop the chills. To-day they are not having them.

I had the headache all day yesterday.   Mr. Wheeler
is complaining of symptoms of dysentery.   I have
been busy in the kitchen to-day, cooking for ourselves and Mrs. Wells.   The kitchen is hung around
with halves of hogs, salted and smoked, which are
called bacon; it is very handy to cut from when
wanted, and on such hot days as this the grease is
dripping from it.   I should think the flies would
trouble it, but they don't seem to be fond of bacon.

SEPTEMBER 13TH.—I never meet a white woman
at the public well.   This is not the place where free
labor is considered honorable.   I meet the black
man and woman—the young man and maiden—the
child;—all are owned by white people, and considered valuable.

I should think that the good people of this little
town never saw a woman dressed in the short dress
before; I seem to attract much notice when I go for
water; I have heard words from a shop near by, that
from their low tone I knew were not intended for
my ear; saying, "O God, look at her! look at her!"
I would say to myself, "O, have I become the occasion for by-words among the people?"

Many of the villagers have called to see us; seem
interested in our behalf; some have urged us to
make this little town our home.   One lady, in a
very friendly manner, has advised me to lay off my
short dress while I remain here, as it is not fashionable.   But fashion and show hold so small a place

in my mind now, that to please a few fastidious ladies for the few days I may remain here, would not
recompense me for the bondage I should submit myself to in wearing long dresses, when I can go so nim-
bly around in my short, loose, and easy dress, to
bring water, pick up chips, bring in wood, milk, *to
get milk,* cook in the kitcken, wait upon the sick,
etc., etc. I have found my present mode of dress
so well adapted and serviceable in every way for the
past three months, that I can well recommend it to
all women who are called to labor or to walk, or who
wish to ramble about for pleasure. Long dresses
will do for afternoons, when all the work is done up,
for drawing-rooms, parlors, and the inactive—but to
energetic, active women, who want to live for health,
and the good that they can do, I would say, don the
Bloomer !

My husband has just found a teamster that starts
in the morning for Boonville ; goes with two teams,
himself and his boy ;—will take us right along; my
husband has tried to persuade him to wait a day or
two, but he cant be put off; so we must be ready to
go in the morning. I am baking bread, and doing
other cooking for our journey.

Our good friend, Mr. Wells, has bountifully supplied us with everything we have needed, and now
refuses any recompense whatever. We have great
reason to be thankful for finding such friends. Mr.
Wheeler is still complaining with an attack of dysentery. Mr. Wells' little child is no better. My

family have had no chills for two days—hope the medicine has cured them.

SEPTEMBER 14TH.—Took leave of our kind friends at the smart little town of Carthage, this morning. When we stopped at noon for the horses to rest, my husband and self got permission to ramble in an orchard and pick up a few apples; they were not mellow, but we roasted them by our camp fire; the children relished them very much. We shall travel a little faster by horse power than we did by ox power. Our teamster has driven twenty-seven miles to-day. Have taken our supper in a house, but shall sleep in our wagon. My family have stood the ride well to-day, but Mr. Wheeler is quite sick; stays in the house.

SEPTEMBER 15TH.—A lovely morning greets us as we start on our way. Mr. Wheeler feels too sick to travel; stops at almost every house to see if he can get in and stay until he shall get better, but does not succeed yet. We are waiting for him now; he is trying again at this nice, looking cottage nestling in among beautiful shade trees. A lady stands on the piazza talking with him; she sees children in the wagon, and here comes a little black girl with a basket of nice, red, mellow apples; she looks smiling as she is bidden to thank the kind lady for us. Mr. Wheeler is disappointed again. We sit in the wagon at this pleasant town of Greenfield, waiting for horses to be shod.

This evening finds us at this, another pleasant little town of Mellville. Mr. Wheeler is very sick; stays in this quiet cottage hotel; my husband stays with him for company. We cannot all afford to stay in a hotel; so our kind driver has driven into this large yard which is attached to the hotel, the gate well locked, and here, under this large, spreading oak tree, I and my children shall sleep in one wagon—our driver and his little boy in the other. My children are asleep; I have been into the hotel administering to Mr. Wheeler; he is indeed very sick; I think he will stop here until he is better. He is very anxious to have us stay with him, but our scanty funds would evaporate like the dew, if we should live in a hotel; besides, my husband and children are very weak; I feel anxious to proceed on our journey that we may get into some sheltered nook, before the fierce winds of winter shall blow. I will crave Heaven's blessing, then try to sleep.

SEPTEMBER 16TH.—We were very sorry to leave our worthy friend Wheeler, this morning, to be sick among strangers; I hope his recovery will be speedy, and soon he will be on his way to friends, as he designed.

Our driver is cooking his dinner of beef stake by a great fire, here at the edge of a pleasant wood. We serve ourselves with our simple food with very little ceremony. Milk seems to be as free as water in this country; nobody will take a cent for all the milk

My Willie is complaining of being sick in his bowels; has some fever; have given him a towel bath, and am careful of his diet.

We find good water here in the vicinity of the Ozark mountains—mostly soft. The land lies in swells; the prairies are small; the wood lands have luxuriant growths of oak, elm, ash, hickory, syca-more, black and white walnut. The crab-apple, paw-paw and persimmon are abundant, as also the hazel, pecan and grape.

We have stopped for the night—yonder's setting sun finds us thirty-three miles from the little town where we beheld his rising this morning. Here is a log house full of children, but the kind folks give part of one bed for myself and my Willie. Mema will sleep in the wagon with her papa.

SEPTEMBER 17TH.—Last night was a lovely moon-lit night—the dark forests to the east of us—the mountains in the distance—the trees, garden, fences, and all objects surrounding the place where we staid were bathed in the moon's light, silver halo; I was up and out many times with my Willie in the bright-ness, when every one about me was living far away in the land of dreams, as quiet as though death had paralyzed every limb; my watchings and anxieties for my child were seen and known by only, as Mil-ton says,

> "Millions of spiritual creatures" who "walk the earth
> Unseen, both when we wake and when we sleep."

We have travelled over rough roads to-day, and have forded the Osage river. The wind is blowing —dark clouds cover the heavens over—and a storm is just upon us; kind people open their door,—we rush in just in time to escape from the pouring rain. I cook rice for my Willie; we take supper with the kind family; they have corn bread, but no wheat bread. Willie says, "please wont mamma let Willie eat the crumbs off mamma's plate?" Precious child! how can I deny him? Still I feel that I must, his bowels are in such a weak state; I must persuade him to eat some of the rice. I learn from Mrs. Cunningham here, that the dysentery prevails all through this country now. It is that disease that is taking hold of my Willie at this time. I shall bathe him and give simple medicine. My anxiety will drive sleep far from me this night.

We behold bondmen and women now, every day; have been surprised to see the care and kindness shown them; most of the northern people labor harder than do these negroes.

SEPTEMBER 18TH.—Have rode all day, sitting on our bed, with but just a trunk to support my back —with limbs extended, holding our darling boy on the dark-colored pillows, which are growing still darker from day to day, from the dust of the roads. As we have passed some very stony places in the road, I have raised my arms, so that my child should not receive any jar.

11

We find comfortable lodgings and kind people to-night—have been listening to a recital of their experience in going to Texas. The old lady says they were all sick there, and forty miles from neighbors, in among the Indians; that when they started to come back, she did not expect her husband would live a day; but as they journeyed he began to gain, and when they arrived here at their old home, he was well. They know how to appreciate the comforts that surround them, and to rejoice that the lives and health of their large family have been spared. Her story gives me some hope; my husband and Mema are better as we journey, but Willie is very sick to-night.

SEPTEMBER 19TH.—Another long day has passed; I feel relieved to lay my sick boy out of my arms on to a bed. We are stopping with fine people to-night. Mema has been with her papa to the dining room to supper; I have taken some corn bread and milk, or nice hoe-cake, baked on a board down before the fire—it has relished well. The negro servant comes into my room and asks if "Missus" wont be helped to something more.

My boy is very sick; takes no nourishment but water. We keep a bottle of fresh water in the wagon as we journey days. I carry him so carefully in my arms that riding does not seem to make him any worse; he seems anxious to ride—I take very little rest at night.

My husband is very anxious to arrive in Boonville; when there we shall reach public conveyance, and on the steamer can have all the freedom we could at our own home (had we one) to take care of our sick boy; and when beyond the Mississippi—when once past St. Louis, we shall speed away to some port, in quick time.

SEPTEMBER 20TH.—Was up at morning's early dawn, making ready for our last day's ride in the lumber wagon. Took leave of our host—took my sick boy in my arms on pillows, and soon were on our way—stopped a short time at noon, and then on we came; arrived in this beautiful town of Boonville just as eventide was spreading her gray mantle over all nature. Our kind but red-faced driver drove through the town down to the river's bank, where he intended to camp.

We had finished our journey in wagons—must leave the wagon that had given us shelter many days—where now should we go to find another shelter? Sick, weak, weary—dirty as we must be, emigrants in reality, after journeying and camping so many days. My husband must go, though weak, in search of a hotel where they would be reasonable, for we must consider our lowering purse, and the mountains still before us. After, I laid my Willie from off my lap down on our bed where his papa had been lying, and told him that we were not going to ride in the wagon any more—that his papa had gone to find a hotel to take us to; he said, "Please lay Willie down and let Willie rest first; Willie's tired."

My husband soon returned; said he had found a good hotel. Our driver offered to carry our sick child, wrapped in an Indian blanket, and soon we found ourselves shown into this little room, made comfortable by setting up a stove, here in Bullock's hotel.

I have laid my little sick boy on to a soft bed, and he is resting his head on white pillows. O, what comforts! what comforts! to the sick, weak, and weary traveler.

My husband has been to the dining room and taken some tea. I thought I would not appear in my short dress at the table, but our young and kind host took me right along—said I must go and have some tea—that none were at the table but their own family. I feel refreshed after my tea.

Mema is sick with an attack of dysentery to-night. We make preparations for retiring—a mattress is placed on the carpet for my husband; my children will take the bed, as it will be more convenient for me to take care of them. It is indeed pleasant for us to be left alone to rest, and make calculations for the future. We have been so long strangers to comforts, and the most common necessaries of life, that we know well how to appreciate the cosiness and home-like feeling that clusters in upon us in this little room—still we are sad, anxious about our two sick children, and wondering how we are to proceed on our journey. We ask heaven's protection, and try to rest.

SEPTEMBER 21ST.—Was obliged to go to the breakfast table in my untidy Bloomer, for our driver had not brought our trunks. All up and down the long table I could see that my dress was attracting considerable attention, by the smiles that played upon the countenances of some, while in others, could see their smiles reproved, as their looks betokened deep sympathy for me. But my care-worn and anxious heart was so much above the sneering world, that darts from such quivers could not reach me. One gentleman's kindness, who sat opposite me, was pleasant at the time, and who, I have learned, is Dr. Hartt, who, with his family, rooms next to us.

I am in hopes that Willie is some better; Mema is quite sick. My husband is enjoying the comforts of this hotel home; though he is paying $2 25 per day, it is low in comparison to the rate at other hotels, and we find this a respectable and well-kept house. We shall be very thankful if our children are well enough to take on board of a steamer in the morning, so that we can be on our way. Willie has been wanting to go on a steamboat; has said many times, "Willie will go home with mamma." But he is too sick now to want anything.

One gentleman boarder has just been in to see us; we find that he once hailed from St. Lawrence county, N. Y.; he expressed much sympathy for us; said he would do all in his power for us, and that we might rest assured that we were among Christian people. I have been obliged to go into the back yard and do some necessary washing for my sick boy, although it is Sunday.

Our trunks have been brought, our clothes changed—I saw no derisive smiles when I went to tea this evening. Mema is better. Willie is quiet; has not wanted to be bathed to-day. I said to him, "you know mamma wants to do everything she can for her little boy." He would say, "*Willie knows mamma does.*" Dr. Hartt pronounces him a very sick child.

SEPTEMBER 22D.—Watched faithfully and alone last night, as mothers are wont to watch; would not allow my husband to sit up with me; knew that he was not able. Willie is very sick—but can't think but what he will get well again. I know his face grows pale, and still paler, from day to day, and his eyes of a more heavenly blue—but we cannot spare our darling boy—he must "*go home with his mamma.*"

Mrs. Hartt has called to-day; seems very kind and sisterly; offers to do anything for me; has sent her servant, who has taken all of our washing to do; I felt that it was too much, but she insisted upon taking it.

SEPTEMBER 23D.—Watched all night,—praying, hoping, fearing. This has been my prayer—"O, grant that I may get my loved ones to some place that I can call home." Mema is quite well again— Willie is no better.

CHAPTER XI.

WILLIE'S DEATH, ETC.

"O Lord, do thou bow down thine ear,
    And hear me graciously;
Because I sore afflicted am,
    And am in poverty."

SEPTEMBER 24TH.—Last night, as the waning moon floated along in her nightly path, and hosts of golden stars added lustre to her liquid light—when all noisy voices and heavy footsteps were silenced by the police, in the streets—hushed was every sound throughout the hotel, indicative of sweet repose—when no sound was heard but the fall cricket's croak, as if instinct whispered, "Autumn is on your track; sing and croak, while you feel a balm in the night breezes, for soon the white frost will lay you a stiffened corse, and your night song, so solemn to the anxious watcher, which notes your short tarry, shall be heard no more;" I sat and watched my sick boy. He was restless and his mind wandering; I thought it might be the effect of medicine; I noted every motion; he yawned, which gave me much hope, for I thought that a favorable omen. As the toll of the midnight hour was on the air, I was sitting by my boy—along as morning began to brighten the east, he called for *white bread, big apples,* and *white corn ;* I thought surely then he was better, for he had not called for anything to eat for a whole week, not since he asked for the crumbs from my plate. I said, "My child is better! as soon as the servants are up in the kitchen I will go and prepare some food for him ;"—feeling so pleased and hopeful, I lay myself down on the bed by his side, (Mema lying on the back side,) and being so weary, and cheered with late hope, I fell asleep. I slept a few minutes only, for when I awoke, the sun was not yet above the horizon; I turned to my sleeping boy; he lay on his face; I put my ear down to note his breathing, but there was no stir in his bosom,—I turned him over, only to see that he was sleeping the sleep of death!—for while I slept, the angels came, and bore him away on their airy wings to their blissful bowers far beyond this scene of struggle, to bloom in Heaven, his natural sphere, without waiting for him to receive father's, sister's or mother's kiss of adieu !

> " Through the night " I" watched " my" darling,
>   Now despairing, now in hope;
>   And about the break of morning
>   Did the angels take him up."

I clasped his little white hands over his heave-less breast, closed his blue eyes forever from my sight, and stood for a time spell-bound before him. Here was the pride of a mother's heart,—her support when her footsteps should totter,—here centered all her bright anticipations of beholding the developement of a noble man, and of feeling the secret and satisfying honor she would feel, in saying all along the pathway of life, "This is my darling Willie,— this my noble boy,—and this my full-grown and manly man!" I exclaimed, "O my God! my God! why is this? my hopes all blasted—my bright anticipations ended—my precious darling boy lies here frozen into marble by the icy hand of death; I'll say, O stern decree! O cruel fate!"

I spoke to my husband, and awoke Mema, saying, "our Willie is dead."

My husband said, "he must have gone without a struggle. I have been awake, knew when you laid down, and was glad that you were giving yourself a little rest after so much watching; thought you were both asleep. Can it be! Oh, can it be!"

After gazing for a while upon our lovely statue, and regaining a little composure from the shock, which his sudden and unexpected release had given, I stepped to Dr. Hartt's door, repeated my sad news, and soon we were surrounded by warm and sympathizing friends, who tried to comfort us with kind words, and still kinder acts. My husband was so overcome, in his weak state, that his chill and fever came rushing upon him. He was helped to Mrs. Hartt's room, and made comfortable in bed; our little treasure was put in charge of our kind, stranger friends, while I sat by the bedside of my weak, sick, and sorrowing husband. Friends came in to consult about his burial; I could have wished to take his precious remains along with us, and have them deposited near where we find a resting place, that I might see fresh roses bloom on the little grave; but my husband's weak state, pecuniary circumstances, and the voice of friends, prevailed; so I consented to let stranger friends robe him for the grave, (I could do it,) shed on it a tear for his mother, and when Spring shall come, plant on it the flowers.

No minister could be had to attend his funeral this afternoon, all were engaged; so no prayer was offered while we stood around the little coffin, save our own prayer of anguish, and no dirge sung, no bells rung. Father, mother, sister, gave the last look, kissed the little cold cheek,—and then in carriages bore the casket away to its final resting place in the city burying ground, a lovely, retired, and shady spot, situated on a slowly-sloping hillside, with other hills rising higher all around, which nature had thickly set with trees, and in among were many large black walnuts, casting their large, lemon-shaped and colored nuts profusely to the ground. The rose, cypress, and myrtle interlaced over many a grave—the wind gently waved the drooping branches of the weeping willow, which bowed over the monuments in a mournful attitude, breathing a soothing requiem as they made up Willie's grave.

We saw the little grave all filled up, evenly sodded over,—gazed upon it again and again; then gladly would I have lingered, but kind friends whispered, "your husband and little daughter are weak, and the night damp will soon begin to fall; come away." So we turned and left the spot, taking another glance, as we passed through the gate, and another as we were handed into the carriages, now bidding adieu, a last and long adieu, to the little mound where our Willie would sleep among strangers!

A number of ladies called this evening, to sympathize with us in this our great bereavement; and we can truly say that the sympathetic tear is very precious.

I have to record here, that the dream of my Willie's sickness and death, was a perfect panoramic view of that of which I have just had the closing scene.

SEPTEMBER 25TH.—We concluded this morning, that circumstances must urge us on our way; as strong as the attraction was to remain, we must break from it, and take our one child, feeling all the time that our Willie was left behind.

Dr. Hartt invited my husband to walk just around the corner of the street to his office, thinking it might divert him some, while I re-packed our trunks to have them in readiness for the next steamer. I folded the little clothes that had been so lately worn, and the suit I had intended my Willie would wear when on board the steamer, to add beauty to his always beautiful frame, and to feed his mother's pride, and laid them down to the bottom of the trunk, not a little dampened with tears that flowed from a full fountain. The last article folded was the little purple sun-bonnet, all dusty, but most precious to me, for I had watched the look of his clear blue eyes so many days, looking up from under it into my face. while riding, when he would say, "Willie feels bad; when will he feel better?" He is better now, but his mother's heart is wrung with anguish.

While engaged in packing our trunks, I thought of the shop a little way down the street, where gravestones were made, and thought how pleasing and satisfying it would be to me if I could sell some of my good clothing and buy some stones to mark the spot where my boy was sleeping. I said to myself, "I will go and see,—for what are nice clothes to me now, unless I can turn them (for I can't pay money) to accomplish the desire of my heart." I accordingly put on my bonnet, took Mema by the hand, and soon we stood inside the shop. I called for the head man, and soon Mr. Bedwell stood before me. I said, "I should like to get some small stones, if you will take some of my clothes which I do not need now."

He looked at me with surprise, as he was evidently eyeing me from head to foot, as if he questioned my honesty. At length he said, "I do not like to take a lady's clothing."

I related the circumstances that compelled me to
ask it, and assured him that he would confer a very
great favor on me by so doing.   He said he would
call at the hotel and look at the clothes. and bade
me select some stones, asking how I would have
them lettered.   I chose some that he would ask nine
dollars for, and said " All I want marked on them is,

" *Willie, the Little Stranger.*"

He assured me that they should be immediately
lettered, and if I did not leave to-day, might go out
to the burying ground with him in the morning
to see them set.   I thanked him, returned to the hotel.   Soon he was here, made a selection, and said
he would send a servant for them in the evening.
When my husband came to dinner, I told him what
I had done; he seemed pleased, and said, " if I do
not have my chill in the morning, I think I can
walk down to the marble shop and see the stones; I
want to, and think I can."

My husband says he has been trying again to-day
to sell his watch, but has failed.   I do wish he could,
for we need the worth of it so much now, to help
us on our journey; besides, he does not feel that he
ought to carry a gold watch in our circumstances;
but the gold watch which has been worn for so long
a time over his heart, and which he has tried so
many times to sell, still clings to us; for what, or

when we shall need the worth of it more than now,
I know not.

SEPTEMBER 26TH.—Last night gave myself up to
rest; for my wearied nature, which had been strung
to the last strain for many days, with anxiety and
sorrow, must embrace the soothing power of sleep,
and for a while forget its care and sorrow, in its ob-
livious rule. But before me, as I slept, floated another singular dream. I dreamed that before our
door here, opening on the street as it does, stood a
long, black carriage; in it were two seats; on each
seat was a person, all dressed in black, and a white
sheep with fleece long and snowy white, making
the contrast great between them and the black carriage and persons dressed in black. The two persons, instead of sitting opposite each other on the
seats, sat diagonally, bringing the two sheep in the
same way. Just as the carriage was ready to move
off, my husband awoke me,—said he was sick; I attended to his call; a cold shudder ran through my
frame, as I noted all the premonitory symptoms of
that dreaded disease, the dysentery; and an audible
voice whispered, " *This is your other white sheep!*"
I said to myself, as I was almost convulsively shaken, "what does this mean; am I to lose my husband as I lost my boy? O, God forbid!"

My husband's chill came on, too, this morning, so
that he was doubly hindered from going with me to
see the little gravestones. I left him in charge of

my friend, Mrs. Hartt, and went to the burying ground; saw the stones set at my Willie's grave, bid the sacred spot another long and last farewell.

Some of the kind ladies assure me that they will plant a weeping willow to droop over the little stranger's grave, and that the rose and myrtle shall intertwine thereon.

This evening finds me watching by the sick instead of being borne along down the Missouri on a steamer as we anticipated.

SEPTEMBER 27TH.—I have been advised by Dr. Hartt and others, to employ a Dr. McCutchen for my husband; they assure me that he will get well under his treatment, adding, that he has the best success in treating dysentery of any doctor in the city. Gentlemen that have called on us, invite my husband to take up his residence here; say that he will find many kinds of business, from which he can choose one that will insure him and his family more than a livelihood. But he has intended to decide what to do, upon our way to St. Louis; if he should be well enough to teach, or to engage in business of any kind, thought we would go up into Wisconsin; if sick, must make our way to friends, and ask their assistance.

Our Willie's death came out in the "Booneville Weekly Observer," this morning. It reads thus: "In this city, on the 24th, Wm. H. Colt, Jr., aged 3 years and 8 months, son of W. H. Colt, of the

State of New York." I have been writing letters and doing up papers to send to friends; have written also to the forwarders in St. Louis, to ascertain the fate of our goods.

SEPTEMBER 28TH.—This has been a long and anxious Sunday. Several gentlemen have been in to see my husband; among the number was one Capt. Walter, who seemed very kind and brotherly. Dr. McCutchen is very attentive; stays every night until twelve or one o'clock, and insists upon my resting while he stays.

SEPTEMBER 30TH.—This month closes with to-day. O, how heavily it has been fraught with anxiety and sorrow to me. I thought when we left Kansas, the first of the month, that before this month closed I should have my sick family safely moored in some place that I could call home. My darling boy has gone home; here lies my husband, I fear, on the point of going home. My lady friends try to comfort me with the hope that my husband will be better in a few days; but there is a voice whispering to me all the time, that I don't like to hear, saying *"This is your other white sheep!"* My heart is heavily vibrating with anxiety. O, my God! "let this cup pass from me."

OCTOBER 1ST.—Went early for the doctor this morning; my husband is very sick; two kind gentlemen will sit up with him to-night. Mrs. Hartt has given up her room to me and Mema. How very kind these stranger friends are.

OCTOBER 2D.—Friends are very kind. My husdand is no better,—is not able to get up—grows weaker and weaker every day; his voice is almost gone,—can converse hardly above a whisper. But the subject of death, and a separation from each other, has always been a common topic of conversation between us; for the reality, which I fear is approaching, has always been a vision that has haunted my dreams. How many times have I been awakened by my much-loved husband, with his asking me what I was weeping for. I would instantly say, "why, I dreamed that you were dead! How could I live without you?" O, my God! is that time coming when all of my dreams will have foreshadowed a reality? How can I,—O, how can I bear to live in that point of time!

I have just been conversing a little with my own best-beloved about going away; he has no fear of death, for himself; feels the assurance that beyond the so-called "dark vale" opens the "pearly gate" to one of his Heavenly Father's "mansions"; but the thought of leaving me and his little daughter in this land of strangers, and in want, grieves his affectionate and noble heart. I asked him what he would advise me to do. He said, "go to your friends; and you know you are to have that insurance money."

Now, as a last request, at this solemn hour, when I am with my beloved husband alone, and while he can speak, I have said, "O, my own dear William, if there is any truth in the so-called 'spirit manifestations,' will you come to me?"

He has said, "Yes, my dear; if there is any law in nature, by the action of which I can come to you, and commune, you may rest assured that I shall make use of that law and come. And now, my dear wife, my Miriam, may Heaven deal gently with you and my child."

OCTOBER 3D.—"The days of affliction have taken hold upon me." O, my God! That dreaded day has surely come; that point of time has made haste; this day has been the day! this eve that point of time! Yes; just after the sun had bid us adieu, and night was hanging her sable curtains round, did my support, my life, my all, bid adieu to earthly scenes, and mount Heaven-ward! I had watched all day,—noted the wanderings of that once strong mind,—wiped the fearful sweat from face and limb, —saw the lamp of life burn faintly, and still more faintly, until it went out without the contraction of a single muscle. I then closed the eyes whose last gaze was bent on me, with my own hand, and exclaimed, "My God! my God! why hast Thou forsaken me?"

Capt. Walter, who was standing by, though I knew it not, laid his hand on my shoulder, saying, "My dear woman, though God has taken your husband, He is able to raise up friends for you."

But O, I cannot be comforted in this hour. When my Willie was taken, I felt that my heart was lifted from its place, and my eyes were a fountain of tears; but now, my whole being is petrified; my breath seems frozen, that it will not come, and I have no tears to flow. My child stands as if bewildered,— tearless. Oh! this is more than we can bear. We must refuse to be comforted because they are not.

The doctor never told me that my husband would die; and why? I could not ask him,—could not bear to hear my doom pronounced by other lips.

OCTOBER 4TH.—I and my Mema arose this morning and went into our room, where lay husband and father, statue like, in the cold embrace of death. I said, "O, my God! my God! can this be a reality; or am I dreaming again, to awake with a shudder,— then to rejoice, and thank Heaven that it was only a dream?"

Capt. Walter called early at the hotel; bade me put my trunks in readiness, and he would send a servant for them, "for," said he, "after the funeral I want to take you and your little daughter to my house, and want you to feel that my house is your home, as long as you wish to stay in Missouri." I thanked him for his kindness; felt that his words, "Though God has taken your husband, He is able to raise up friends for you," were being made true. Parcel after parcel was handed into Mrs. Hartt's room for me, even to a paper of handkerchiefs, and I soon learned that the kind ladies were fitting me out with mourning. O, such kindness and thoughtfulness is balm to this deeply wounded heart.

Afternoon came. The ceremonies of a city funeral were held at the hotel; then the hearse moved slowly through the streets, then along the quiet, retired, and shady road that leads to the silent resting place of the dead, followed by two *true mourners*, and a few sympathizing friends. Then was committed to the grave my support, my life, my *guiding star!* Oh! language is too feeble to describe the deep anguish that was smothered deep down in my heart; so deep that my whole being was paralyzed with a mountain's weight of bitterness, as I heard the pebbly dirt rattle down upon the coffin's lid—it seemed to me as though all nature was being rolled together, and I the only one left to hear the dismal sound. I would have bowed over the two mounds forever, but a voice, weak, sweet and low at my side, said "Mamma." It touched the only life cord, and thrilled my heart with a strong and life-giving desire to protect, guide, and love the one that yet called me "Mamma."

I find myself and my fatherless child, on this sad night, under the hospitable roof of the very pleas-

ant and refined home of Capt. Walter.   Mrs. Walter seems to be a most excellent and warm-hearted
lady; and it seems to give the whole family pleasure to administer comfort and sympathy to us, the
afflicted.

This seems almost too much of refined life for me
to come in contact with at once, when I have of so
late been obliged to live almost as rude a life as
though I had lived in the red man's wigwam. Then,
how can I bear to step on these soft carpets, partake
of the dainty meal, and rest my wearied nature on
this soft and snow-white bed, when my beloved husband and darling boy were called away so soon by
death, before they had hardly tasted of the comforts
of civilization?

Ah! my husband's dream comes to me now, when
he said, "we traveled until we came to a great river;" and so we did,—the river of death. He has
taken one child, and has passed over into life,—immortal life—while I remain here with the other. O,
why could we not all have struggled in the dark
waters of "Jordan" together, and all have come out
on "Canaan's fair banks," and have been a happy
family,—not separated.

OCTOBER 6TH.—

> "I look around, and feel the awe
>   Of one who stands alone."

This sorrow-stricken heart of mine would naturally give up to the corroding influence of silent grief; but circumstances that surround me bid me arise, and give my mind at once to business and preparations for the future.

Have received a letter from Simmons & Leadbeater, forwarders in St. Louis, saying that the goods have been sent up to Kansas City. My friends here think it best, (as my goods must be sold to pay freightage,) for me to go to Kansas City, and attend to the sale of them myself; keeping my books, and selecting the articles I wish to retain. But my child is very weak; she cannot bear to be away from her mother a moment; it would be cruel to leave her, even with such kind friends, who are willing and anxious to care for her; and it would be exposing her delicate health too much to journey there and back, the distance of four hundred miles, on a steamer, with drinking the Missouri water; neither can I bear to make the journey myself, unprotected, now in these troublesome times. So many dangers and sore trials have beset my path, that I have but little effort to put forth, and had rather lose everything I have in Kansas City, than to bring one exposure upon us two, who are now to move over the world's dark waters alone. My kind friends tell me to keep my husband's gold watch, and not part with it on any account. Another friend, Mr. Williams, tells me to take no thought about my bill at the hotel, that he will see that it is paid; then my late husband's funeral expenses have all been paid; his coffin was

$20; it was covered with black velvet, and mounted with silver-plated screws.

The kindness of these my stranger friends, in these my necessitous, trying, and afflictive circumstances, strikes upon a vein of gratitude in my heart, which otherwise I would not have known was there. And could they know the volume of gratitude that wells up from my heart to them and to Heaven, for their kindness and sympathy to *this deeply wounded heart*, and for administering to my necessities, they would say, "It is more blessed to give than to receive."

And now, after all they have done, they offer to raise any amount necessary to take us to our friends; but I am glad to say, that after all my bills have been settled by their kindness, I think I have enough in my possession to take us on to our friends.

OCTOBER 7TH.—This week the county fair is held in this city. I have been invited to attend, but have too dark a shade of sorrow thrown around me, to have a desire to go where the joyful will meet, and and the gay put on their gayety.

My friends have devised a way to have the sale of my goods attended to without my going to Kansas City. Mrs. Dr. McCutchen has a brother, Dr. J. O. Boggs, residing in Westport, Mo.; A. B. Coffey has a friend residing in the same place, Col. A. G. Boone. These two gentlemen it is thought best to appoint to attend to the sale of said goods. As all the goods were marked in my husband's name, it has given me a long and a very descriptive letter to write, to describe the contents of the boxes, so that my goods can be taken and sold, and father Colt's reserved for him. I also had to write out a list of the articles I would like to have reserved. I have written in great haste in order to send by this night's mail. It has overtaxed my brain, for I feel one of my hard headaches coming on.

OCTOBER 9TH.—All day yesterday I suffered in my room with a severe headache. My Mema, the while, amused herself by going into the flower garden and gathering seeds, bringing them into our room and doing them up in papers to be packed away in our trunks, and in making rag dolls. It has seemed to me, all through my sojourn in Kansas, and my journeying thus far, that I have been upheld by a power and sustained by a strength beyond my own; but now I feel like Sampson shorn of his locks; I have become weak, my strength has departed.

Friends advise me (and it seems also necessary) to reduce my baggage, as I should be obliged to pay extra with so many trunks, and besides it would make so much care for me when I come to travel alone. So I have concluded to have the clothes of my dear, departed husband sold at auction, (Oh! how can I bear it?) and to use the avails in purchasing grave-stones for him, so that I can also mark the spot where HE lies sleeping. Accordingly, I have folded each precious article, which seems an embodiment of his own true and noble self, have taken a farewell look and filled a trunk to the overflowing; the trunk was a present from my father, and still bears the initials of my girlhood, but it is too much worn with this season's travel to bear any more hard usage, so it must go too.

Soon a servant is to be sent to take these precious garments to the auctioneer's stand, where clothes are sold, and there every article which I would press closely to my heart, is to be held up to receive the bids, then struck off to the one who bids the highest, scattered to the four points of compass, and worn I know not by whom! Ah, ah, ah; this is aggravating in the extreme,—but I must submit. It is like probing a fresh wound with a red-hot iron, but it must needs be.

"My heart is sore pained within me; and the terrors of death are fallen upon me,—

"Fearfulness and trembling are come upon me, and horror hath overwhelmed me."

OCTOBER 10TH.—Have been to the marble shop, and selected the stones for my husband's grave. They are to be lettered with his name and age, with the addition of this line,

HERE SLEEPS MY HUSBAND, BESIDE MY DARLING WILLIE.

Stones that would be sold to others for twenty-two

dollars, I get for eighteen. Friends seem anxious for me to remain in Booneville, and I feel riveted here —cannot bear to think of leaving the spot where my two treasures lie buried. Have hinted that if I could get a place as governess in a family would stay; and now a friend assures me such a place is open for me, if I will accept it, in a fine family of seven children, where I and my little girl will be well cared for, and I remunerated with eight dollars per month. I shall think upon it.

Mrs. Hartt has fitted my all-wool delaine dress; I sew all the time I get from writing letters and attending to other business; my dresses will soon be finished. Several kind ladies have called on me to-day; sympathy, to my sorrow-seared heart, is like rain drops to the drought-parched earth,—and may they be bountifully rewarded for weeping "with those that weep."

OCTOBER 12TH.—This has been a most lovely day; the rich autumnal sun has bathed this lovely city, the fields, woods and glens, with his bright crimsoned light; heating down through all the mat of leaves on the garden vines, as if meaning to ripen all the last set fruit, before the heavy frost shall come. The family have all attended church; I staid with my Mema, who is not very well. We have walked in the orchard, where the trees are bending with most delicious fruit, and the full ripened and golden corn is ready for the harvest. We have walked in the vegetable garden, and the garden of vines, where now the melons and tomatoes enrich their vines, as yet untouched by frost; then in the flower garden, where blooms many a modest flower, and many very rich and rare.

The negro servants belonging to this fine establishment, Peter, his wife Harriet, and little David, have been away since yesterday to attend a daughter's and sister's wedding. They came home just at night full well loaded with wedding cake, which was passed around in whole-souled pieces. I never saw cake that looked nicer, or that tasted better. Peter gave me a fine paw-paw; it was as large as a medium sized long potato, bluish, with large flat seeds imbedded along in the rich meat; it resembes the muskmelon in taste, only much richer.

The negro slaves here have a very easy servitude I should think. The kitchen, which stands a few feet from the house, seems to be a palace to them; in their private rooms, joining the cook room, stands their curtained bed; a carpet is on the floor; the mantel piece is ornamented with lamps and vases, and many keepsakes; while on one side of the room hung in sight Harriet's silk dresses, much gayer and more costly than those worn by her mistress. All of these Peter gets by improving the time that is his; and when his Harriet, his "ole woman," is dressed in one, he thinks there is not a negro woman around that surpasses her in beauty of form or feature.

The negroes are all out here on Sunday nights, as happy as all Africa when the sun goes down ; but when the nine o'clock bell rings, then there is a scampering heard in every direction homeward.

I have attended church this eve, leaving my puny child with Mrs. Walter. And now, this hour of ten, finds us in this large, pleasant square chamber, where we can overlook the most of the city from the balcony. My Mema is wrapt in sleep. Yonder's untired moon, veiled in a halo of silver mist from the air of this balmy autumn eve, is pouring in a flood of heaven's own light at my window, as if anxious to light up a heart overburthened with dark sorrow, with the light of hope, of which her own pure and mystical beams are an emblem.

"And perchance thou art casting this mystic spell
    On the beautiful land of the blest,
Where the *dear ones* of earth have departed to dwell,
    Where the *weary* have fled to their rest.

Oh yes ! with that soft and ethereal beam.
    Thou hast looked on the mansions of bliss,
And *some spirit*, perchance, of that glorified world,
    Hath *breathed there a message* to this.

'Tis a mission of love, for no threatening shade
    Can be blent with thy spirit-like hues,
And thy ray thrills the heart as love only can thrill,
    And while raising it, melts and subdues.

And it whispers compassion; for lo, on thy brow
  Is the sadness of angels enshrined,
And a misty veil, as of purified tears,
  Round thy beautiful form is entwined."

OCTOBER 13TH.—W. W. Gill, editor of the Booneville Weekly Patriot, (in which is a notice of my
husband's death,) has sent twenty-four numbers to
me; I have them done up to send to friends. The
notice reads thus:

DIED.—In this city, at eve of the 3d inst., WM. H. COLT, son
of John G. and Mary Colt, of the State of New York, aged 40
years, 3 months, and 3 days. The deceased leaves a wife and
one little daughter to mourn his loss. As a husband, he was
devotedly attached to his wife,—and a kind and indulgent
father."

        My Father and my God:
Teach me if hope, if joy, be mine,
To bless Thy bounteous hand Divine;
And still, with trembling homage, raise
The grateful pæan of exalted praise!
When deep affliction wounds the soul,
Still let me own Thy mild control;
Teach me, submissive and resigned,
To calm the tempest of the mind;
To lift the meek, adoring eye,
Suppress the tear, and hush the sigh;
Gaze on one bright, unclouded star,
And hail "the day-spring" from afar—
Bid angel faith dispel surrounding gloom,
And soar, on cherub wings, beyond the tomb.—ED.

I have decided to leave Booneville; my husband's voice whispers in my ear, "Go to your friends," and my heart yearns to meet kindred again, and to behold familiar faces; although strong cords and friendships bind me to this lovely place. I must obey *that voice.*

OCTOBER 14TH.—That trunk full, and more, of precious clothing has been blown to the winds; and I received twenty-six dollars, a paltry sum for so much good and nice clothing.

Mr. Bedwell calls, and takes me in his carriage to the resting place of the "much-loved dead," to see the stones set at my husband's grave, and to take a long and last farewell.

> Two graves are made here, side by side,
> In one's my hope, the other my pride;
> I leave them now, and say farewell,—
> To steer my barque on life's lone swell.
>
> Yet, when I wander far away,
> Here my lone spirit oft will stray;
> At morn, at noon, at silent eve,
> I'll sit me here—in sorrow *grieve.*
>
> How can I say, "Thy will be done,"
> When all's so dark beneath the sun?
> The cup 's been rais'd—the dregs are drain'd;
> A life I've liv'd—I'm sorrow stain'd!

OCTOBER 16TH.—Have been to the office of Joseph

L. Stephens, with Drs. Geo. C. Hartt and Jos. E. McCutchen, where they have made affidavit to the sickness and death of my husband. The papers are all made out, and I shall send them to R. Wood of Montreal, (where my husband's life was insured,) agent of the Conn. Mutual Life Insurance Co. I have to record the kindness of J. L. Stephens in making out said papers for me free of charge; for which I am very thankful.

I believe my business is done now, in this place; my trunks are packed again, and have taken leave of the most of my friends; am waiting to hear the word, "the steamer Russel is here—make haste or she'll be off!"

CHAPTER XII.

The waters are deep now, the waters are deep;
　My *Life-boat* has gone from the lee;
O, who will protect from the tide in its sweep—
　Will JESUS be out on the sea?

OCTOBER 19TH.—Friday we sat, as it were, with bonnets on, to be in readiness for the steamer, for they make short stops, and Capt. Walter's was more than one-half mile from the river. Just as the sun was hiding himself afar off down behind the distant horizon, and night was hanging her gray mantle over all scenery, coloring it all the time to a darker shade, and memory busy in picturing to the mind's eye the depth of sorrow that had flowed into the already desolate heart just at the same hour two weeks ago, when the dusky hues of night were coming on, the word came, "The Russel is here!" Then the command was given to the servant, "Hurry with the baggage!" and the word, "the carriage is at the door." The last farewells were then spoken, and we hurried away to obey the call of duty, when a cord of cable size would not have held the soul's affections, and body with them, from the pleasant little town of Boonville.

The steamer moved, breathing heavily, down the river; I gazed upon the place we had left with thoughts unutterable, until a bend in the river, and the deep shade of night shut from my view, no doubt forever, the spot most dear to me of all on earth.

When seated in the saloon, my Mema said, "Mamma, it seems just as though we had come away and left papa and Willie, and they were feeling bad." Ah, how natural the supposition.

There are many very pleasant ladies on board, and one feels a radiance of warmth in associating with Southern people, so that when the hand is extended it is a surety that the heart is not far off. The steamer has just passed Alton, where the bright waters of the Mississippi flow in with the "dark Missouri flood," and side by side they roll on for miles before they will venture to mingle. This is a very bright afternoon; all the scenery looks familiar—the trees are clothed in as green a dress as when I looked upon them last Spring,—no frost has tinged them with richness yet. Flocks of wild ducks light on the sand-bars, and when the steamer ploughs along near them they are frightened up, but soon light upon the sand-bar again. The cars have just passed—the track runs close along by the river; they are going from Jefferson City to St. Louis. We shall soon be there.

OCTOBER 21ST.—Sunday eve, as soon as we went

into St. Louis, crossed over the river and took the cars for Chicago; rode all night and all day yesterday, until four o'clock P. M., when we found ourselves in the great city of Chicago; changed cars, procured tickets for Jackson, Mich. Arrived in this city at three o'clock this morning. Came immediately to my brother-in-law's,—Albert Foster's. It was pleasant to look upon a face that had been seen before. All seemed rejoiced to welcome us, the widow and fatherless, to all the comforts of a happy and refined home; and although my own dear sister had, many years ago, gone to her reward in Heaven, I found her place well supplied by a good sister Hannah.

I rode from Chicago to this place without holding up my head, it ached so hard, and so I have been obliged to keep my bed all day; I feel better tonight; have visited some, but am now in my room again to rest.

OCTOBER 22D.—Have been riding with friends, all about this fine city; have visited the cemetery, where, among the sleeping dead, lie some of my own kindred. Have been to the State Prison; went into its chapel, workshop, eating department, cookroom, and cells; saw hundreds of prisoners at work, dressed in their roundabout stripes; heard the wailing and self-condemnation of the raving maniac, whose crime had been murder. Truly, "the way of the transgressor is hard," when man condemns and punishes. O, when will mortal man look upon all mankind as brethren, and the so-called prisoner be looked upon as a diseased person demanding pity instead of as a culprit deserving condemnation?

The Democrats are having a great torch-light procession to-night; great excitement about the Presidential election.

NOVEMBER 6TH.—I returned from Parma, the distance of fifteen miles, on the cars, two days ago, where I had been to visit a brother whom I had not seen for years. What joy thrills the soul when severed members of the same family meet; tears flow as gems of gladness, upon receiving the tender embrace of love; the memory of early days sweeps over the whole frame like an electric shock, painting a full panoramic view of childhood scenes, when we were gathered, "like olive branches," around the same paternal board; receiving alike the "well done," or the rebuke of parents. Then the spring-time of life is talked of, and lived over again,—and we fancy for a moment that time has not led us out from the sheltered cove on to the broad sea of life, rocked our frail barques with the howling winds of blasted hopes, nor shipwrecked us with the keen tempest of sorrow.

My Mema has been sick a number of days with a slow fever; so I have my place by her side day and night, watching the disease, and nursing and administering to her wants. With the advice of friends, the homeopathic physician was called to see her yesterday, so she is under his treatment, while I have the privilege of giving her all the water treatment I choose. O, I hope my last, my all, will not be taken from me!

NOVEMBER 15TH.—Received to-day the following letter:

OFFICE OF CONNECTICUT MUTUAL }
LIFE INSURANCE COMPANY, }
HARTFORD, Oct. 30, 1856.

MRS. WM. H. COLT,—Jackson, Mich:

MADAM—Your letter, with certificate of physicians, to the death of your husband, W. H. Colt, is received at this office, but is not sufficient to establish a claim upon the policy. We require the certificate of the sexton or officiating clergyman, and of some person who was acquainted with your husband, to identify him as the person insured by that name.

Respectfully yours,

GUY R. PHELPS, Sec'y.

Have written to Booneville, and to St. Lawrence Co., N. Y., for the proof required at the insurance office, besides several letters to friends.

Mema's slow fever has taken the intermittent form—chills and fever; she is very weak,—requires much care. My friends are very kind. Yes, the sympathetic balm is still poured upon the sorrow-crushed heart.

"No radiant pearl, which crested fortune wears,
 No gem, that twinkling hangs from beauty's ears,
 Nor the bright stars, which night's blue arch adorn,
 Nor rising sun that gilds the vernal morn,
 Shine with such lustre, as the tear that breaks
 For others' woe, down virtue's manly cheeks."

NOVEMBER 29TH.—Have just received a letter from friends in New York, containing very sad news about the friends that were left in Kansas. It seems that after we left Kansas, father Colt was taken with the congestive chills, and died very suddenly and unexpectedly, in the third chill, (as they most always do,) at eve, just as darkness was beginning to brood all over the Kansas prairies. Mother Colt and sister L,, although weak and feeling sorely afflicted, watched alone with the dead husband and father through the long, dark and gloomy night, when the dismal howl of the prairie wolves could be heard all around and in the distance, as they traversed the dark landscape—and the chill prairie wind came sighing mournfully in between the chinkless logs and at the blanket door; while nestling about between the stones of the floor, and under the loosened bark of the logs, were scores of crickets and katydids, pealing forth their nightly songs, thinking, perchance, to soothe and while away the long, unmeasured hours; while to the watchers, theirs were the notes of the funeral dirge. The looked-for morning at length dawned; then kind neighbors came in and dressed the cold form of the departed for the grave.

They nailed together some of the rough "*punchuns*" he had taken from the wigwam ruins, for a coffin, wrapped him in a winding sheet and Indian blanket, and laid him therein; then bore him away without prayer, requiem or knell, and laid him in his narrow home beneath the rich soil of the prairie, on whose bosom were still blossoming many a rich-tinted flower. His grave was made a little south-west of his rude dwelling, (the centre octagon,) where the oak and walnut trees scattered out from the woodlands on to a lovely prairie swell, inclining to the northward, just enough to make a cool and pleasant shade, and which was known to the Company as "Sober's place." He was not laid ·there to rest alone, for all around were marks where the earth was treasuring the red man's bones. ·

Mr. Stewart took the widow and fatherless to his own home. It was thought, for many days that mother Colt would not long survive her husband's death; but she began to be better, and was very anxious to start for her Northern home. Henly, who proved himself to us to be a Border Ruffian robber and extortioner, told them that we were in Missouri, in order to get their cow, calf, tools, other utensils and money besides for taking them to Carthage, where he left us, and where he told them they would find us; when he knew very well we intended to journey right along. When out in Missouri, they were very much disappointed in not finding us, but were determined, with their failing strength and

means to go northward; they thought they might
as well die on the road as where they were among
strangers. Disappointment, sickness, sorrow, and
almost despair, gave energy to the weak, excited
nerves, and they hastened on. The same man that
took us to Booneville, carried them to Jefferson City.
The hand of charity was extended, and the feeble
mother carried from car to car by strong men. The
same evening that I and my child went into St.
Louis on the steamer, they, mother and daughter,
too, went in on the cars. So near each other were
afflicted friends, and yet knew not what had befall-
en each other. They journeyed on, and on the 27th
of October arrived in Stockholm, St. Lawrence Co.,
N. Y., at a daughter's and sister's.

On the 4th of November, mother Colt bade adieu
to all the scenes of mortal life, and joined the other
members of the family, who had a few weeks before
entered upon the confines of the unseen world. It
was only for a few days that she rested from the
anxiety of traveling, reposed upon a downy bed, enjoyed the fresh linen, and received all the attention
of a sweet and loving daughter, who would have all
tread softly, that the wearied and sick mother might
rest. But thank Heaven for the few days she was
permitted to look up into loving and familiar faces,
and receive the kind welcome from old neighbors,
and after receive a Christian burial, and be laid beside those of the family who had gone years before.

Often father Colt would say, when we urged him

to leave Kansas with us, "I had as lief lay my bones
in Kansas, as in any other place;" and so it has
come to pass. But to think of a death in Kansas,
in that wild though beautiful country; to be laid
away in a rough box, in a grave marked only while
the mound looks newly made; away from all kindred and friends who would drop on it a tear, or
plant on it a flower, seems to me horrible in the extreme; and it gives me a melancholy pleasure to
think that my husband and child died in a land of
civilization, where for a fews days they had the comforts of a tidy room and bed, and pillows on which
to rest their heads as the curtain of life fell, and
ushered them into the spirit land,—where they could
have pure cold water right from the fountain, and
enough of it too, to quench their feverish thirst. I
could wish that our dead might be gathered up and
laid side by side. Surely, we have been a "doomed
ship." The words of the Psalmist are upon my
lips, "O Lord; rebuke me not in Thy wrath; neither chasten me in Thy hot displeasure; for thine
arrows stick fast in me, and Thy hand presseth me
sore."

DECEMBER 19TH.—Mema has had a very hard chill
to-day; it seemed as though she would shake all to
pieces,—and so it has been for many days past; she
would be shaking when the little girls came home
from school at noon, and other members of the family came to dinner. Then the question has been

asked so many times, "How is Mema?" My answer has been, and is, "O, she has another hard chill!" until I can hardly bear to have any one ask me how she is. I continue the same treatment. She lies so quiet and still nights that many times in the course of the night I hold my ear close down to her chest, to listen for her breathing. I tremble with fear and anxiety about her, lest I may soon have to part with her. My friends are more than kind ; they are indulgent—their kindness I can never repay—may Heaven recompense them for administering to the wants of the poor and afflicted.

My Mema has been sick (with the exception of a few days at a time, when she has taken medicine to stop the chills,) since last June.

DECEMBER 22D.—This is Mema's 10th birth-day ; she missed her chill yesterday, and has also missed it to-day ; seems much better ; I do hope they will leave her now to get well.

I have received many kind and sympathizing letters from friends of late, which send a wave of joy o'er the troubled waters of my sea of life, to think there are many noble hearts that remember me.

DECEMBER 27TH.—For a few evenings past have had the privilege of attending O. S. Fowler's lectures on the very interesting subject of phrenology. I have long been anxious to hear Fowler, having read so many of his works. Called on him at the hotel, and was introduced to his very intelligent lady—had a very pleasant time.

JANUARY 5TH, 1857.—For a number of days this live city has been all alive with gayety, pleasure and enjoyment of the holidays. Old Santa Claus has been round and round, making sparkling eyes, and bringing out merry laughter from the little folks, upon their seeing what beauties, what sweets, and what oddities the old gentleman kept stored away in his "leather pockets," to rattle down the chimney into their stockings. Nor has the mirth been confined to the juveniles alone, for many an older face has brightened with joy on beholding some elegant Christmas or New Year's present, said to have come from out the "leather pockets." Then has come the calling together of dispersed families and friends, to gather around the richly supplied board, partake of all its dainties, and have warm and loving hearts more tenderly bound together. The lately-made widow and fatherless have not been forgotten in the distribution from the "leather pockets," visits, rides, and sumptuous fare of the season; but more than all I have enjoyed the return of health, that imprints itself upon the face of my child from day to-day. Have to-day received the looked-for letter from Booneville—I will note its contents.

BOONEVILLE, Mo., Dec. 6th, 1856.
MY DEAR MRS. COLT—Some time has elapsed

since your letter was received; I have been truly grieved that I have not been able to get your business done, until within a few days. Mr. Walter was not able to get the gentlemen together in order to have it done according to law. He has now forwarded the papers to the Insurance Co., as directed.

I was much pleased indeed at the reception of your letter, as so long a time had elapsed without hearing of your safe arrival. I had felt anxious in regard to you. I am very glad you are once more among your friends, as you will naturally feel more at home than you would among strangers, after your *very sad* bereavement, but am sorry to hear of the sickness of your *dear little girl;* hope ere this that her health is entirely recovered.

There has been a great deal of sickness in the hotel since you left. Your friends, who are many, so far as I know, are well, and often inquire about you. My family join with me in sending much love to you, and your child—we shall be pleased to hear from you often. May God bless you and yours.

                                        M. C. WALTER.

Another letter has just been placed in my hand; it is from sister Mary Colt Everts, of Stockholm, New York. She announces the death of sister Lydia Colt. She died the last day of December. In the short space of four months, five, of seven in a family, have passed on through the shadowy, misty path that veils from the vision of mortals the glori-

ous view of immortality. They have gone home—
"HOME *to die no more;*"—myself and child are
permitted to tarry yet a little longer, to feel all the
loneliness, gloom and sorrow that encircle the be-
reaved heart.

"The dead, the much-loved dead:
　Who doth not yearn to know
The secret of their dwelling-place,
　And to what land they go?
What heart but asks, with ceaseless tone,
For some sure knowledge of its own?

*　　*　　*　　*　　*

Grief cannot win them back;
　And yet with frequent tear,
We question of their hidden lot,
　And list with throbbing ear,
For some low answer that may roll
Through the hushed temple of the soul.

We love them—love them yet!
　But is our love returned?
Is memory's hearth now cold and dark
　Where once the heart-fire burned?
Nor do the laborers now gone home,
Look for the weary ones to come."

JANUARY 21ST.—Arrived here in Owasso to-day;
find my nephew, B. W. Davis, and his lady, well.
The weather is very cold; we have had good sleigh-
ing since the 20th of November;—I see no difference between this winter in Michigan and a Montreal

winter—cold and with deep snow alike. I and my
child have journeyed with and by the kindness of
friends, across the country, eighty miles, from Jackson to this place. Have had a good, long, and very
pleasant sleigh-ride; staid one night in Lansing, the
Capital. The State Legislature is in session, and
the town was so full of people that Mr. Carpenter
(the gentleman we journeyed with) looked a long
time to find a vacant place in one of the hotels,
where we could stay. We stopped one week in
Bingham, near St. Johns, where we spent the time
very pleasantly, visiting with old acquaintances;
they then brought us to this place. I like this part
of Michigan—it is a general level, but with eminences
sufficient to give a pleasant variety of scenery—fine
flowing rivers, with lovely valleys. It is timbered
with beach, birch, oak, maple, aspen, and walnut,
which grow very large, tall, and straight; but just
as we enter this town there begins to be a little
sprinkling of pine, just enough to make the forests
look dark and warm for winter; but not far north
of this place, the woods darken into dense forests of
pine, where much lumbering is done.

This country looks new but thrifty; when riding
through the woods we would all of a sudden come
right upon a thriving little town, made up of white
cottages as clean as the drifted snow around them,
scattered in among the stumps, the contrast adding
beauty to their neat and tasty architecture; such are
Lansing, Dewitt, St. Johns, Mason, etc., all growing

like vegetation in summer-time. But the prettiest of the pretty, is this little Owasso, (*bright spot*) as the Indians called it, beautifully situated on the Shiowas river, Shiowassee County, and noted for its grand water-power. It is a young town, but very flourishing, as well as pretty and "*bright.*" The "iron-horse" goes snorting through here many times a day. This railroad is to be built on from St. Johns, where it now terminates, to Lake Michigan.

JANUARY 25TH.—In two or three days have received a number of letters, as tokens of remembrance from friends—one from Mr. Edward Childs, who was formerly one of our Montreal friends, now residing in Toronto; when I opened it, out dropped, and fell at my feet, a ten dollar bill. I thought of the old adage, "A friend in need, is a friend indeed." May Heaven reward him! it was received with a thankful heart.

I meet old acquaintances in this place, whom I have not seen for many years—not since I parted with them on the shore of Lake Champlain, when they stepped forth into the world, bound for Michigan, which then was thought to be the "far West."

My relatives are doing much to make me happy while I tarry with them; we are going, or receiving company, almost every day, which is diverting for the time, and my heart is full of thanks to them; still my heart is sad, and a loneliness pervades my being, "every where I roam." O, who but the wanderer and the homeless can understand all the meaning that is *volumed* in the one word *Home ?*

FEBRUARY 24TH.—Have to-day received a letter from the Life Insurance Co., as follows,—

HARTFORD, Feb. 16th, 1857.

Mrs. WM. H. COLT, Owasso, Mich.—Yours of the 10th inst. is received.   There is nothing more required of you to perfect your claim on policy insuring the life of your husband, and we are ready to pay it, and have been since it was due on the 1st inst. upon discharge and surrender of the policy. * * * *

Respectfully yours,

GUY R. PHELPS, Sec'y.

and have written to Montreal for my policy, where it was sent last spring to have the premium endorsed by R. Wood, agent of the Life Insurance Co., and in care of M. Babcock, a friend. When my husband sent it, he did not know what the amount of the premium would be, and did not send enough to pay it, so it had to be retained until the whole was paid, consequently he did not get said policy before we started for Kansas.

My Mema is improving in health from day to day, and enjoys herself very much with the little girls she meets here and there while visiting.   As there are no children here for her to play with, her cousin has found a stray, half-starved, and half-frozen kitten at the barn, and brought it in for her to pet. It looks rough and forlorn; she imagines it is sick, so she is trying her skill to-day in the healing art,—it has enjoyed the comfort of a warm soap-suds bath, and a dish of yarrow tea stands handily by, and very often the little caterwauler is forced to take a teaspoonful.

MARCH 13TH.—A letter from friend Babcock has just been placed in my hand. He says, that on the 4th day of last August, according to my husband's orders, he mailed said policy, enveloped, with money, to Neosho City, Kansas Territory, via Fort Scott.

So now comes another dilemma. What is to be done? Surely the Fates are about my path! I knew nothing of the orders my husband gave for the policy; and he was so very sick in his last illness, that I conclude he forgot to mention the fact. Previous to our leaving Kansas he wrote to the postmaster in Fort Scott, to send his mail to West Stockholm, New York; so that if all was right, I should have had some tidings of the wanted policy. I have no doubt but that the envelope was broken open, the money taken, and the policy destroyed somewhere on its way. Have just written another letter to the Insurance Co., giving them an account of the loss of the policy, and asking their advice. This is the twentieth letter I have written in regard to this insurance business.

It shall be my endeavor not to be too much cast

14

down in viewing the dark clouds of adversity that seem to be gathering in my horizon; but may I remember that Infinite Wisdom deals out the destiny of mortals, and He will give only what will be for my good. I have already been showered with many more blessings than I could have asked, since I deposited my *Treasures* in the lonely city of Booneville. Of a truth, I have found *Jesus out on the sea.*

MARCH 26TH.—Two days ago came another letter from the Insurance Co; it reads as follows,—

HARTFORD, March 19th, 1857.
Mrs. WM. H. COLT, Owasso, Mich.:

MADAM—Your favor of the 13th inst. is just received. It is very unfortunate for you and embarrassing to us, that your policy is lost—unfortunate to you, because as it is the only evidence there is of the claim, it could not be collected without the policy—and embarrassing to us, because we want a voucher for the payment, and a protection against any future claim by the policy; which it is difficult to get otherwise than by the policy itself. We do not and cannot know but the policy has been assigned to some other person; and if so, then we are subject to be again called upon for payment, though we should now pay it to you. We are not at all disposed to take any advantage of the lost policy, nor to delay the payment in consequence of it, but it is

proper we should have such a discharge of it as to
protect us hereafter from all liability or trouble
therefrom. But the great difficulty is, how can that
be done? The nearest approximation to a remedy,
is for you to make affidavit that the policy is gone
out of your possession, by being as you believe *lost;*
that it has never been assigned or transferred to any
person, but is now your property. And as there is
some apparent informality or incongruity in the
manner the insurance was taken, being taken by you
in the name of "Miriam Davis," wife of Wm. H.
Colt, it will be necessary for you to explain in the
affidavit the whole matter, by stating that you are
the widow of Wm. H. Colt, deceased, whose life
was insured by policy No. 9424, issued by the Connecticut Mutual Life Insurance Company, dated
May 6th, 1850, and that you are the person described
in that policy, as "Miriam Davis," wife of Wm. H.
Colt, and that the insurance was effected through
the agency of Robert Wood, of Montreal, by you,
for your own benefit—and in signing this affidavit,
you had better sign as you did in the application,
"Miriam Davis," widow of the late Wm. H. Colt,
deceased.

In addition to this affidavit, we must have your
bond, with some responsible persons as surety, in the
amount of $3,000—conditioned that you covenant
with the Connecticut Mutual Life Insurance Company to guaranty and defend said company against
all claims and demands by reason of the said policy,

and to hold them harmless from all liabilities by reason thereof. The bond should state as the explanation, that the policy (describing it) is lost, and gone from your possession, but the amount claimed by it has been paid by the company.

The preparation of these papers may make you some trouble, but we cannot do with less and be protected. It will be necessary for you to get some lawyer to draw them up, who will understand what is necessary if you detail what I have written, and state the circumstances of the case to him.

We shall want the certificate of some third person, that your surety is responsible for the amount of the bond. With these papers correctly made and executed, and the addition of your discharge of the policy in form, as enclosed, we shall be willing to pay the amount due ($1,959 13) upon receipt of the papers.   *   *   *   *   *

Respectfully yours,

GUY R. PHELPS, Sec'y.

I have been to a lawyer; have had the required papers made out, and the bond signed by A. H. Byerly, a very wealthy gentleman of this little town, and B. W. Davis, my nephew. I cannot express my gratitude in words to Mr. Byerly for stepping up like a good brother and aiding me, a stranger, at this critical juncture, to obtain what is my due, and what will give a livelihood to me and my child. Mr. Byerly has sent the papers out by express to-day.

MARCH 27TH.—My good niece, Jenny, other friends, myself and Mema, have been to Mr. Hinman's, visiting, and to eat warm sugar. The day has been bright and lovely; from the fast melting snow, little brooks have purled in every direction; such sunny days point one on to the time of singing birds, young and tender leaves, and budding flowers; when they say, "Owasso will be a bright spot in-indeed." We enjoyed our walk very much there and back on the railroad, stepping from tie to tie, to show our dexterity; but we enjoyed our visit more with the two very pleasant Mrs. Hinmans; then came the new warm maple sugar, which was very nice indeed.

APRIL 4TH.—Was "up town" to-day visiting a friend, when Mr. Byerly (the Express agent) came in where I was visiting and placed a package in my hand. I opened it—when was presented to my view the whole amount of money for which the life of my husband had been insured: a thousand thoughts rushed into my mind, and the tears could not be kept in their fountain, but would trickle down my cheeks in spite of the effort at self-command which I was making. I thought, "It is just six months to-day, since I saw all that was mortal of that beloved husband laid away to rest in the cold bosom of Mother

Earth, far from any kindred, only the precious **Wil**-
lie that was sleeping by his side." I thought, "how
pleased he always seemed to be to keep the premiums
paid on the policy, so as to have the insurance secure, saying, 'that is for you and the children, if anything should happen to me that İ should be taken
from you;' and when about to be released from the
clay, when his limbs were paralyzed with weakness
—just before his calm, strong, and noble mind began
to wander—and when his voice was lowered to a
whisper—it seemed to cheer and comfort him in his
weakness that he had made such a provision, when
he whispered," " You know you have that insurance
money."

It is precious to me far beyond its moneyed value,
for I feel that it is the "price of blood"—the life
blood of that beloved husband—garnered for this
one day of need. I hope I shall have wisdom to
invest it, and to use it with economy, that it may
subserve the original design.

I cannot be thankful enough to my friends for
their assistance, to the insurance company for the
honorable and gentlemanly manner of dealing with
me, nor to God for His guidance in it all.

APRIL 8TH.—With the advice of friends, have
rented the greater part of my money at 10 per cent.
interest, taking mortgages for security, on land. I
have been in this pleasant "bright spot" of a town
almost three months; have made many acquaint-

ances, and feel very much attached to them; cannot leave without feeling a sadness at heart at parting with friends, who have manifested so much kindness and sympathy: they will long be remembered by me. Have said farewell to them all, and shall leave in the morning on the six o'clock train for Jackson, via Detroit.

APRIL 9TH.—We were on the cars by the time this morning—hastily passing through a new and somewhat rough part of Michigan, but which is to become a fine country. At half-past ten a. m. the cars stopped at the depot, in the large city of Detroit. My nephew, who had accompanied us thus far, took us to the Waverly House, to wait for the train going west. We amused ourselves until dinner was called, by looking down into the street at what was passing there—fashionable ladies, richly arrayed in brocades, feathers and furs, would pass along; then the beggar girl, with tatters streaming in the breeze, would follow in their wake; then would come the business man, the lawyer, doctor, student, clerk, and perchance the minister; and then would pass the sewing girl, the servant maid, market boy, old lady in rusty black, dray-man and black man; and then a man in form, who would reel from one side of the street to the other, complaining all the time of the streets and buildings moving. After dinner, we attended the exhibition of sewing machines in an adjoining parlor. We took tea; then it was announced

that the train was ready. My good nephew then
waited upon us to the cars, bade us good bye, then
waved his hand in token of good wishes, as the
whistle was blown and the train started off. The
sun was down soon, and the night shut from our
view the delightful country through which we passed.
After another ride of 80 miles, and at ten o'clock,
we found ourselves here in Jackson, at the white cottage of my brother-in-law, Albert Foster. We are
welcomed back with many kind greetings, and much
chatting has to be done. Now, in this pleasant
chamber again, it looks home-like, and seems to bid
the tired rest.

APRIL 15TH.—Attended the sewing society of the
laidies of the Methodist church, with sister Hannah,
to-day. It was well attended by fine, intelligent, energetic and benevolent ladies, whose whole hearts
were engaged in their work of benevolence. I enjoyed being there as well as I could expect, for this
has been a day of review with me. It is just one
year to-day since our family, all well, started for
that far-famed Kansas; the whole sad picture has
swung before my vision all day, rolling in upon me
like the dark billows from the troubled ocean. The
past year has been to me one in which has been
gathered enough of dark shadows for a life time;
rolled up and condensed to make the darkness still
more dark, and the sorrow deeper and more over-
whelming.

MAY 2D.—Within the past two weeks have visited my brother again at Parma, and old acquaintances in Spring Arbor and Marshal, whom I have not seen since the days of my girlhood—in the morning ing of life—when hope was high, and the heart was young. It is pleasant thus to meet old friends, to go back in years and for a while forget one's griefs, in living again, in fancy, beneath skies that had no clouds for the future, where the bow of hope ever spanned the heavens,.and where not a rumble of distant thunder was caught by the ear's quick and sensitive tympanum, to hint that in the distant future lay hid the seeds of storms, dark and furious.

MAY 18TH.—Left Jackson, the 11th, at five o'clock P. M. My dear, good friends accompanied us to the cars, and put us in charge of those that were coming East. We bade farewell again, and off on the lightning train we sped our way, past marshes, little lakes, fine farms, pleasant villas, and handsome cities and over sparkling brooks, meandering through a fine undulating country, dotted with groves, sparse woodlands, church spires, and beautiful habitations. At eight in the evening we arrived at Detroit, crossed the river, and rode all night, through Canada, on the Grand Trunk Railway.

At five o'clock A. M., on the morning of the 12th we came to one of the world's wonders, the Suspension Bridge at Niagara. Here we were delayed a few hours in consequence of a train running off from the track, which gave us time to view this grand work of art. displayed in the mechanism of the Suspension Bridge, and the sublime work of nature in the Falls of Niagara. Who can stand on the trembling earth, and look at the waters from the great lakes pouring over the rocks of ages into the unfathomable abyss below, foaming, sudsing, sparkling, spraying, and describe it? Able pens must fail if they attempt it; then let mine be still. Wonder, sublimity, ideality and language, are all frozen into a state of inertia while viewing the grand scene, amid its roar and mist. After a little, these words may be breathed from the lips, and vibrate on the ear: "Marvelous are Thy works; and that my soul knoweth right well." We walked down and up the 300 stairs, then back again along by the precipice, two miles, to the cars.

I did not hold up my head riding from Niagara to Syracuse; then was obliged to leave the cars and go to a hotel, and stay two nights and one day, suffering with a sick headache.

Arrived at Potsdam at five o'clock P. M., on the 14th, at my eldest brother's, where we were received with many warm greetings. Made a short stop in Potsdam, visiting friends; and now to-day finds us in West Stockholm, at brother Hiram Davis's. We are also welcomed back again here by many; here resides my aged, widowed mother, and here we expect to abide.

I would now thank my God for His watchful care

over us, through the dark and howling storms of adversity and sorrow, when all were shipwrecked and lost save us two. We have rode on the waves of life, and are now safely moored in our old town, near friends, and only seven miles from where we embarked on that ill-fated Kansas Expedition.

MAY 22D.—Have bought of my brother the five acre lot, almost opposite his house, and entirely disconnected from his farm; have paid him $200 for it; intend to build on it a very small cottage, so that I can have a little home of my own, be near my mother, and claim a brother's protection.

MAY 26TH.—Intend to work on my five acre farm all I can, in order to be economical, improve my health by being in the open air, and to try and dispel the dark clouds of sorrowful thought that would overwhelm me if unoccupied. I have done very well, part of the day, in taking my first lesson in planting corn.

Last Winter I wrote a letter to the postmaster at Grand Rapids, where resided a brother of friend Wheeler, whom we left sick in Mellville, Mo., to see if I could learn if he was in this mortal world. I have just received a letter from said Wheeler. He says that after we left him he was very sick for many weeks,—suffered all he could and live. Says, " My pen shall never tell what I suffered." He is now at the Water Cure, in the western part of this State, "trying," he says, "to get the drug medicines out of my system."

JUNE 10TH.—Leafy June; singing birds, and fields of many shades of green have come; from mother earth spring blade and leaf from all the seeds that rest in her bosom, causing man to look forward with hope to the coming of a plentiful harvest. I have planted .potatoes, beans, peas, and many garden seeds.

Although I am no architect, yet I have drawn the plan of my little house, and the builders are engaged. Have received a letter from a friend; it reads thus:

BOONEVILLE, Mo., April 1, 1857.

MRS. WM. H. COLT:

Esteemed Madam—I received a letter from you, of March 28th, several days since, and a note from Col. A. G. Boone, of Westport, in reference to your goods, and have this moment received his reply, from which I extract the following sentence: "The goods have, or a part of them, sufficient to pay the expenses, been sold; and the remainder shipped to the lady, according to her instructions." I regret very much the delay in the matter, but presume it has been deferred on account of the river and all means of easy and safe transit being closed during the Winter. I was truly gratified to hear from you, and that you had met with kind friends. Wherever your lot may be cast, if it be among the good and true, they will be friends of yours. It is a matter of regret with us that we were unable to do something of real merit for you; but when the heart is riven, and the sun of hope seems set in the ocean of bitter disappointment, and the cup of joy dashed with grief, then human sympathy is mockery, and God, the Father, the only ark of refuge to which we can point, or from whom derive consolation. We who had the privilege of knowing you, feel ourselves benefitted by the lesson of meekness, and firm confidence in Providence; and of true and noble womanly devotion, which we witnessed in your tender love for those who sleep beneath the turf of our little city.

With the hope that you may never want for kind and loving friends, and that the Dispenser of every good will keep you faithful and true, even unto the end, I am, madam, with the highest regard, your sincere friend and well wisher,

A. B. COFFEY.

Another letter in regard to my goods.

WESTPORT, Mo., April 12th, 1857.

MRS. WM. H. COLT:

Dear Madam—I have just received your letter, giving directions in regard to the shipment of your goods. I received your former letters, one from Booneville, the other from Michigan. I wrote to Mr. Coffey in reply to the one received from Booneville, and would have replied immediately to the one from Michigan, but for want of information from Kansas City at the time. Previous to the reception of your former letter from Michigan, I had made sale at public auction of such articles as remained after making the reservation you requested at first— Mr. Coffey having instructed me to do so, saying, if they did not sell for enough to pay the charges he would pay the deficit himself. They sold for much better prices than I anticipated, bringing within three or four dollars of enough to pay the charges. The deficit being so small, the commission merchants at Kansas City, Messrs. Reiddleburger & Co., kindly agreed to make you a present of it, and also to keep the goods until the opening of navigation, and ship them to you without any further charge. They applied to me about the first of March for directions in regard to shipping, and I gave them as contained in your former letter. * * * I suppose they have been sent, and have probably arrived at their place of destination before this. I sold the little tea-kettle you mentioned; but knowing the gentleman who bought it, I called upon him, and he readily consented to let me have it back. You will therefore be gratified in your desire to have it. The other little articles you mentioned were sold, and not knowing to whom, I could not get them again. My services in this matter have been a pleasure to me, and the consciousness of having, even to this trifling extent, rendered you any assistance in your

afflictive circumstances, is a sufficient reward. * *
I shall be very glad to hear that your goods have
reached you safely, and shall feel anxious until I do.
Write to me again when you do receive them; or if
you fail to receive them, let me know.

Yours, with respect,

JOSEPH O. BOGGS.

How great the kindness has been from every one
since I stood up in the world alone. I thank Heav-
en for it.

JULY 4TH.—I am visiting in the neighborhood
from whence I started for Kansas. All the neighbors look as natural as when I left; every house,
tree, stone, stump and log occupies the same place;
even the chips in our old door-yard seem to be all
there, and look precious to me because my Willie
used to tread them so often, and pick from them for
his mamma to make a good fire of to cook his papa's
dinner. Every nook and corner of the old farm are
the same, and for a moment seem to allure me with
the thought that my own beloved husband and father Colt are busily at work somewhere on the farm.
The little house, and flower garden in front, fain
would say that mother Colt and sister L. still keep
it tidy; train the drooping vine, and smile at the
opening of every new flower.

This has been a day of national rejoicing; the
booming of cannon has been heard in every direc-

tion.　Near here there has been quite a fine celebration; the tall liberty-pole, with the stars and stripes streaming from its top in the pure air of Heaven, has betokened *Liberty !* when, to me, a sable banner would be more appropriate, as it would proclaim the bondage of thousands.　I declined joining in the festivities of the day, for my heart is very sad; memories of the last Fourth have flitted before me all day; and now, at this late hour I am inclined to bid my thoughts to roam away to the Land of the blest, and the beautiful lines of Bulwer are on my lips:

I.

" When stars are in the quiet skies,
　　Then most I pine for thee;
Bend on me then the tender eyes,
　　As stars look on the sea.
For thoughts, like waves that glide by night,
　　Are stillest when they shine,
Mine earthly love lies hush'd in light
　　Beneath the heaven of thine.

II.

There is an hour when angels keep
　　Familiar watch o'er men,
When coarser souls are wrapt in sleep—
　　Sweet spirit meet me then.
There is an hour when holy dreams
　　Through slumber fairest glide,
And in that mystic hour it seems
　　Thou should'st be by my side.

III.

The thoughts of thee too sacred are
  For daylight's common beam;
I can but know thee as my star,
  My angel and my dream!
When stars are in the quiet skies,
  Then most I pine for thee;
Bend on me then thy tender eyes,
  As stars look on the sea."

JULY 27TH.—The cellar is made, and the frame of my little house raised; the sound of the hammer, saw, and other tools is heard there early and late. My goods from Kansas City have come safe to hand, for which I am thankful. They are our clothing that was boxed, some bedding, and little choice articles, with my husband's books, which I prize more than all the rest; their value to me cannot be estimated by dollars.

A letter from Kansas has also been placed in my hand:

NEOSHO, Kansas, May 17th, 1857.

DEAR MRS. COLT:

Yours of March 30th was but recently received. We had thought and spoken of you very often, and at every mail hoped to hear from you. But did not, until a short time before receiving your letter, hear of your great bereavement; Mr. Voorhees then wrote to us of it. Be assured, Mrs. Colt, you have our tenderest sympathies in this, your great affliction—bitter indeed has been your cup. What a

15

destruction of family in one short year!—how soon our fondest hopes may all be crushed, crushed!

To us the past year has been one of many hardships and troubles, but our lives have been spared, and since about the time you left we have enjoyed good health. We have got things fixed up around, so that now we live quite comfortably.

Samuel (our brother who went to take Clubb to Kansas City) got home the evening after you left, in good health. He had some narrow escapes, and to get home was obliged to go around through Missouri, one hundred miles out of his way. * * *

Mr. Adams went shortly after you left to Maysville, Arkansas; we had a letter from them in the winter; their health had improved. The Broadbents both died shortly after old Mr. Colt. Mr. Hobbs went back to Ohio. Mrs. Barker remained with us until late in the fall, then went to Kansas City with the intention of going home. Buxton is still in the neighborhood. Blackburn went to Tennessee, home to his family.

Emigration is coming in very fast, and we are getting many new neighbors. There is a town laid off up the river five miles, and a steam mill is to be put up there this summer. Altogether, the prospects for us in the future are encouraging.

Mrs. Stewart has a son, born April 8th. She is very well. The past winter has been quite mild—the spring is backward.

We would be gratified to have you write soon again. Receive our best wishes for your future.

Respectfully, your friends,

WATSON AND LIZZA STEWART.

OCTOBER 17TH.—Time is ever on the wing, however sad and lonely the heart may be. Autumn is visiting this latitude with rainy days, frosts, and bleak winds, premonitory of snow and the colder winds of winter.

My little cottage, the building of which I have been superintending, is now ready for its occupants, and to-day I and my Mema have moved into it. Its dimensions are 19 by 29, with a piazza in front toward the west, and a wood-shed 12 by 16 back toward the east. Only two rooms—both in front, with each a door and a French window with blinds, opening on to the piazza. The living room or kitchen is 16 by 12, with a bed press, kitchen closet, pantry—which is made partly in the wood-shed off from it—one large window toward the north, and one in the bed press, which can be let down at the top for ventilation, besides the French window in front. My parlor is 12 by 12, with a bed press, a nice cupboard for my precious books, a large window toward the south, and one in the bed press, also the French window in front. Up stairs I have two pleasant rooms and one large closet all furnished. A place is left below in the partition between the rooms to set a stove, so that one little stove warms the whole house. I have had my house built for comfort and simple neatness, not for fashion or elegance. It is well painted on the outside with white. My kitchen and pantry wood-work I have painted with a tinge of the first dawn of morning; my little parlor I shall paint white.

It seems very strange for us to be in a house alone; it is as still almost as the grave. It is raining hard, and all the noise I can hear is the water running musically into the cistern in the cellar. Shall have plenty of soft water to pump up into the pantry, and shall know well how to prize it too. I have provisions stored in a large, deep cup-board that opens into the wood-shed, where not a mouse can get to nibble.

We have helped to harvest our corn and potatoes, which are put in the chamber and cellar for our present and future use. The beans are shelled and put in a bag, and good and mellow apples scent the cellar.

December 15th.—My small barn is furnished, and "bossy-cow" is snugly ensconsed in her warm stall. The part that our poultry will occupy is finished after the model of the late style of heneries. The fence, that will enclose one acre of ground and divide it into two parks, to keep the "biddies" from roaming, is being built six feet high with pickets. The half dozen Bramah chickens, that Mema brought from Michigan in a four quart wicker-basket on the cars, (causing great wonderment to all on board,) have grown to crowing roosters and laying hens, and we have bought fifty more to live with them in their new home; I intend to keep 200, so that we shall have some business suitable for our rural home.

Altogether, my little home is costing me some over $300 more than what I expected, and what I brought money to pay; but my interest will soon pay it. I have given, and shall give my notes so as to meet them along as I get my dues. Was to receive interest every six months; the six months were up the first of October, but on account of the hard times this year the men have sent only $15; they are in hopes to send more soon. I was intending to get some plain, necessary furniture for my house, but in consequence of my money's not coming, have been obliged to pick up the cast-away bedsteads, chairs, etc., and paint them over, and must make do for the present.

DECEMBER 31ST.—So far this is not a severe winter to go out in to do the chores of a man. We find our little home warm and handy; have the necessities of life supplied, for which I know well how to be thankful; but living by ourselves we miss husband and son—father and brother, more it seems than when in the bustle of other's houses.

As this has been the last day of the year—and this eve the last eve, it seems a fitting time for retrospection; and as only a few days ago I entered upon my fortieth year, I can go back a long way in thought, review my path all the way along up, and now let my thoughts rest for a little on *The Widow's Home* and *Heart*. Months have passed away, and still he comes not. The widow's heart is still bleeding from the deep wound that has been made, and which still seems to be incurable. Everything around seems draped in a darker hue since he whom she loved so well is gone. Even the moon in her silver brightness and the sun with his golden rays seem dim, compared with the days when her heart was cheered by him who was her pride, her hope, her "polar star." The sable garb is still kept on—colors would not be in unison with the mourning of the soul. Still she must try and appear cheerful, and not darken the path-way of other mortals; for what good would come of letting the world know how often every passing day and season is reflected back with a cutting smart upon her own sad heart, as she stands up in the world *alone*.

She beholds many manly faces, both in public and private, but her heart asks—where, O, where is the one that smiled on me, and the arm that gave to me protection? Glad days come and go, when husbands gather up their wives and little ones, and hasten to their friends to enjoy a rich repast and social chat. But a tear gathers in her eye, and her heart seems too big to be carried in her bosom, as she endeavors to appear bright, and wishes all much joy.

When the comfortable meal is made ready, and the chairs placed around the table, the place opposite hers is vacant, and no word is given to call him who once graced that place.

When even-tide comes on, and everything is done up for the day, and that which she was not wont to do is done, when the blinds are closed—the world shut out, there is no listening to hear his footsteps fall lightly at the door; no anticipation of his coming still later, and no expectation of seeing the door open, and of hearing that well-known voice say, "*Well, here again*"—no, no! The evening must be spent in lonely thought, or an effort be made to get interested in some work or book that will seem to to make the sands drop faster and faster until the time for retiring shall come. But sleep seems to be at a distance—thoughts acuter grow—view after view of the past revolves before her—thought after thought, hope after hope dies again—fear after fear darkens, until at last she loses herself in quiet sleep. Then that eye, which ever beamed on her with affection, and that arm, which was ever ready to protect her, is with her ; and as she nestles to his side, and hears again that voice that was wont to say, "I love you," she is happy.

Morning comes—the vision's flown—she sighs and says: "How can I, O! how can I live?" But the departing voice whispers as it recedes, " You have one left—live for that one."

CHAPTER XIII.

MY EARLY LIFE, ETC.

Then go with me where the mountains range,
    And their summits meet the sky;
Where cliff and the craggy rock are seen—
    And a creek goes surging by.

There, too, where a lovely lake is seen,
    Where waves wash its pebbly shore;
Beside it I entered on life's scene,
    Where unknown was all before.

In merry childhood's innocent glee,
    How soon do the years pass by,—
Then gaze to the future—ask for me
    What's in my life's destiny?

March, 1858.—

My dear friend, Mrs. Voorhees, as you have expressed the wish for a peep into my history, previous to meeting me on board of the steamer Cataract, at St. Louis, bound for Kansas City, I will gratify you in that desire.

There is nothing of what the world would call noble or renowned in my pedigree; and there was all in surrounding circumstances, that would tend to hold a mind down that was dependent upon outside influences—I mean poverty in my generation; yes, my father was poor; so I was not born with a silver spoon in my mouth, or nursed in the lap of luxury, or heir to an estate, only by rumor. My pedigree is traceable to the West of England, my estate to the city of Bristol, and my nobility to honest, good-natured grandfathers and grandmothers, who dwelt in the town of Chesterfield, N. H., "the Old Granite State." There lived and died my grandfather, Ezra Davis, who married Amy Snow; there, too, lived and died my mother's father, Capt. Benjamin Smith, and his wife, Louis Bacon. My father's name was Darius H. Davis; he was born in Chesterfield, N. H., on the 6th of Nov., 1785. My mother's name was Louis N. Smith; she was born in Chesterfield, N. H., Aug. 5th, 1785. My parents emigrated from their native town, and settled at Crown Point, Essex Co., N. Y., when that was called a great distance from the old New Hampshire State, in order to keep their growing family around them in a new country. My father was a mechanic, a tanner; moral, upright, and strictly honest in all his dealings with his fellows. His integrity of character far outstripped that of those of much greater pretensions; his pleasantness, cheerfulness, and submissiveness to an overruling Power, cannot be equaled. The memory of my dear, departed father is pleasant, and I often dream of seeing him in all his wonted goodness. Yes,

"The departed! the departed!
    They visit us in dreams,
And they glide above our memories
    Like shadows over streams."

My father was too confiding to be very shrewd in business, too noble to stoop to the "grab game" of the world to enrich his own pocket; so if he had by hard labor a few hundred dollars laid up to enlarge his business, the eager and dishonest were, by some game, sure to get it; hence, poverty and toil were his.

My mother was ambitious, economical, benevolent,—a true wife and kind mother; but has been a great sufferer for more than fifty years, with the phthisic; I fear her lamp will soon go out.

Well, it was in Crown Point, on the 18th of December, 1817, on a cold winter night, (while my father had gone to the city of Troy on business,) that I, the twelfth of seventeen children, entered, two months in advance, upon my mundane life. No one but my fond parents thought me worth raising, so no amount of care and nursing was too much to lavish upon their little, weak child. When five weeks old, they ventured to tie me up in a red silk handkerchief, and hung me on to the hook of the steelyards, when, to their encouragement, I weighed *six pounds;* my blanket was shaken when I was wanted, then I would drop out.

Time sped on; the baby grew,—and at two years

old, can remember that a little brother was sent into the family to hold the most prominent place there. Since that time memory has served me in recording the events of my life. Our homes were many; school at a distance, and I was too puny to attend, consequently learned to read from the older children. When eight years old, remember of trying to go to school some, and of reading in the renowned English Reader, and spelling in Webster's Spelling Book. These were all the books I had to study, (for it was but little I went to school,) until I was fifteen years old; then I became the owner of Smith's Grammar, and a share in Olney's Geography and Adams' Arithmetic. I was very anxious to learn, but from ill health, caused by our living in a malarious district, I had had the fever and ague all the previous Summer; and now it would not leave me able to attend school but twenty-four days during the Winter. My kind teacher offered to call at my father's to hear my lessons, but I was not well enough to study.

Previous to this, for a number of years, I had attended Sunday School, and always kept at the head of my class, reciting from Bible question books. I wanted to be good; so, as I thought, made my "calling and election" sure, and united with the Congregational Church before I was fourteen.

At the age of fifteen, I was anxious to dress well, as all girls are, and my father was able to get me but a very few clothes; so I agreed to work for a brother's wife, at 25 cents per day, enough to buy a calico dress that would cost 37 1-2 cents per yard. I washed at home on Monday, and on Tuesday for my brother's wife. I had the dress, a pretty light one, and just like our minster's wife's; surely, I thought, it would be nice to go to church dressed like our revered minister's wife, but was not able to wash enough to pay for it all. I was the oldest one at home at this time; my two sisters and two brothers, of the many older than myself, were all that were living, and they were married and away before I was fourteen.

As I viewed my father's circumstances, I knew that I must make my own way in life—go out and take care of myself; so the height of my aspirations were to attain to the position of school teacher, and I hoped that some day I should have a pair of scissors hanging at my side, fastened with a large scissor hook to my silk apron strings—have a green silk calash bonnet, and green ribbon to hold it over my face, and walk to and from school with a score or more of little urchins calling me school-ma'am; this would constitute my beau ideal of attainments and honor.

What caused me to shed many tears in my early life, was that I could not have the opportunity of getting an education, and I almost coveted the advantages that some girls had of being sent away to attend an academy school; so I would wish that my father was rich enough to board, clothe, and pay my tuition, somewhere at a high school. But what I crave must be gained by my own effort; I felt a determination to clothe and educate myself.

The winter I was sixteen, attended our district school; my mother needed me the Summer after. My seventeenth Winter boarded at a brother's, attended a district school, working nights and mornings, besides one day in each week, to pay for my board. I was obliged to keep very busy in school and out, to get my lessons in the three common branches, (for I was a dull scholar,) and pay for my board. I could not think of much recreation, though I believe I did go to one sleigh-ride.

The Summer after, I kept house for my eldest brother, who had some months before been called to part with his good wife, and lay her mortal remains in the tomb, leaving him to mourn, and two little daughters motherless. I maintained my place as housekeeper, with all the dignity I could command at this early age, until another took my place and was called mother.

Shortly after, my youngest brother, a cherub of five Summers, was stricken with the scarlet fever, and was laid soon in the church-yard. This was a great grief to us all, and we deeply mourned for him. The nine that had been taken from our family before, were all taken in infancy. Now ten of us had joined the angel choir; one brother and one sister were left younger than myself.

Attended the three months district school the

Winter I was eighteen, and the Summer after, I had the honor of being school-ma'am in one of the back districts of my native town. I did not wear the green silk calash, but a shaker, made of brown muslin smoothed over a pasteboard frame; it was very fashionable; besides it kept the sun out of my face, and was very genteel for a school-ma'am. I taught for 75 cents per week; was not obliged to be inspected, as they had had a qualified teacher in the Winter,—and should not have merited a certificate if I had been. But I kept my school out and gave good satisfaction, so they said. After my school closed, I sewed on their sewing and quilted at one place; did house-work for an acquaintance the Winter I was nineteen; ought to have attended school. The next Summer was applied to to teach in a part of our town known as "Hell's kitchen;" had one dollar a week for teaching in a district bearing such a hot name. I liked my school, my boarding places, enjoyed my walks back and forth from school, through the woods, and was not any too warm. I heard of no dissatisfaction, save from one woman, who said, (because I punished her girl,) "I'll send her where corn is cheaper." She soon felt better; I kept my time out, and was wanted to teach there again. I was not inspected this season, so dared not engage the Winter's school. The Fall found me just across the lake, spinning wool.

The Winter I was twenty, I did house-work in a hotel for a very estimable lady, a kind friend. She gave me $1,25 per week. While with this lady I learned many a lesson in housekeeping, which has been of great value to me. By being very careful and tidy, I could now dress as well as other young ladies of our town ; and with my emulous organization I must be, else I should have felt mortified and mean. Happy are those who possess a large share of self reliance, and can hold up their heads even though clothed in rags.

The Summer after, I taught school in one of the first districts in town ; was obliged to study to keep ahead of my large scholars ; learned more that Summer than I should if I had attended school. In the middle of the Summer went before the School Inspectors with trembling and fear, it being the first time, and I knew my knowledge of the elementaries was very little ; but I soon heard, by the by, that our good minister said I bore the best inspection of any he had inspected that season. His saying that gave me much courage. After, he visited my school ; approved of my mannnr of teaching, and advised me to make teaching my business. This again strengthened my weak confidence in self, and the more as it came from my pastor, shepherd of the flock.

The winter I was twenty-one, was prevailed upon to teach through the month of December, in order that the district might draw their public money, as their summer school had been taught by an uninspected teacher. I was paid two dollars per week, and wanted the rest of the winter, but I had made up my mind to visit with my parents my grand-parents, whom I had never seen.

When ready for our journey, heard that there was no snow in Vermont or New Hampshire, and being determined to have a sleigh-ride, turned our course toward this St. Lawrence county, where the snow was white and deep. My eldest sister was coaxed to journey with us—leaving her little family for a few weeks—to rest and regain her health, which was poor.

We journeyed through what was called " the woods;" we saw that our provision boxes and pails were well filled with baked meat and beans, boiled chicken, ham, the best of biscuit, butter, doughnuts, cheese, mince-pie, and a variety of cakes; so when we put up at a log hotel, we furnished our own ta-ble, calling for cup of tea, and paying for our trouble. We had a gay time visiting our friends in St. Law-rence county, then went to Fort Covington, Franklin county, to visit a rich uncle, Mr. Allen Lincoln, whose riches did not cause him to feel superior to his poor relatives. Both uncle and aunt (she being my father's sister) entertained us with the best that their large and well filled house afforded; while I enjoyed myself very much in the society of, and had many a pleasant ride with, my cousin Allen M. Lincoln, who was pleasing in his manner, and about my own age. This kind uncle offered to help my father to a tannery situated in Parishville, St. Lawrence co.; thought he could find good business there.

My father, mother and sister went back home, leaving me in Fort Covington. I spent three months there very pleasantly. When my uncle went to New York on the first of May, I went along with him, riding in the stage coach and on steamboat back to my native town;—for me I had made a great tour.

In three weeks after my return home, my father was ready to start for St. Lawrence county. Two double wagons held our goods, our family of five, and two drivers. Our way was through the woods again, but winter had gone; the road wound up over mountain and hill, through valley, over plain, across the rushing stream, by craggy rock and over-hanging cliff, along beside the quiet little lake, and over the murmuring, pebbly bottomed brook where scores of speckled trout were sporting in the clear, sweet water. A late, new growth of tender leaves clothed the maple, beach, birch, ash, poplar, and linden; shrubs were white with blossoms, and many spring flowers were peeping through the mat of dried leaves. The odor from all the freshness of spring, mixed with the balsamic smell of the tall giant pine, hemlock, spruce, cedar, and sweet fern of the plains, gave us a rich perfume to inhale all the day long, and which the dampness of night seemed to condense and furnish in greater abundance. Romantic, healthy, and wild indeed was this journey.

We arrived at our destination in Parishville, St. Lawrence county, on the first day of June, 183 9

16

My sister Louisa, six years younger than myself, in a few days went to live with our good aunt in Fort Covington.

Somewhere on the journey, without our knowledge, we had come in contact with the contagion of measles; my brother and sister did not have them very hard, but they nearly took my life.

We found Parishville a very pleasant, quiet village, situated on the St. Regis river and environed with wild and romantic scenery, which to a poetic mind would give sentiment for many a verse. A fine agricultural country spreads abroad from it. My father's business was good here, and in two or three years we made improvements, so that we had a tidy, pleasant home, a plenty of the good things of life, and could receive and treat our friends without that feeling of mortification which poverty always gives to the proud heart. I spent many pleasant and happy days in this little ville, in the society of the friendly and large-hearted.

The Fall after we came to this town, I got able to teach a very pleasant, juvenile select school for three months. The Winter after, when twenty-two, attended the village district school. I studied hard, but made slow progress, for I needed to apply myself closely to study in order to acquire a little knowledge. The next Summer I taught the village school on the other side of the river, (there being two districts in the village,) in what was called the old Academy.

My twenty-third year I attended the village school part of the Winter, then went with my father and mother on a visit back to my native town. The Summer after, attended the Academy school in Fort Covington—paid my own tuition—boarded with my friends. These four months finished up my school-going days. Went to Parishville in the Fall, fitted as I hoped to teach a Winter school; was soon applied to, to take the school in the old Academy. I had a large school, some days numbering seventy; taught four months, and when the pay-day came the trustees paid me more than they agreed to, which was proof to me that I had given satisfaction. The other school was taught by Wm. H. Colt, until he had an application to go to Montreal, Canada, to teach a government free school in connection with the American Presbyterian Church; then the school was taught by a young lady.

I continued teaching in Parishville village and vicinity until the Spring after I was twenty-six, 1844; I then had an unlucky tip-over out of a sleigh, which badly hurt my left side. I was subjected to a course of doctoring—taking emetics of a carbonate of potash obtained from blue flag roots. Thus were the functions of my stomach almost destroyed. I have lived since that time by using the greatest amount of self-denial in submitting the good things of life to my stomach for digestion; and what would be called temperance in eating to most of folks, to me would be intemperance, even to extinguishment of the life spark. So my fare must be the plainest and coarest, as I journey on through life.

In these years there would often come the "white-winged messenger," from the British Province of Canada, laden with accents of love, true and tender, from an affectionate, noble and manly heart;—once in a long time a visit instead.

In the Spring of 1845, in a little house in P——, and in the "sanctum" chamber room, were many kinds of sewing hurried along; light silk, white muslin, were carefully concealed from the observant eye; a bonnet with the slightest tinge of salmon, ornamented with delicate white flowers and silk lace, was kept with the lid of the band-box on, down on the under shelf in the deep cupboard. All the rooms in the house were put in order save the kitch-en—there was heard the pulverizing of white sugar, beating of eggs, preparing of fruit, and these much anxiety, (lest we should not have good luck,) until the pyramid white cake with snowy frosting, the fruit cake wreathed with sugar plums, and the cup cake blushing like fresh roses, were placed side by side on a table, and received the epithet, nice! nice!

On May-day, fathers, mothers, brothers, sisters, and a few friends, were gathered into the plainly furnished, but neat parlor,—then the holy man stood up,—while the white muslin fluttered from the beating of the timid maiden's heart as she took the mar-riage vow,—and closed by saying, "What God has joined together, let no man put asunder." After, came congratulations, large slices of cake, dinner, tears at parting, a ride in a stage coach, on steamer and cars, and then in a cab up to the door of a large boarding-house in the city of Montreal, where I, as Mrs. Colt, was welcomed to Canada.

The next day was Sunday; I was seated at the head of a pew in the American Presbyterian Church, and this seat in church was mine for the seven years that I dwelt in the city. Verdant country girl as I felt myself to be, I was introduced into the society of the well-educated, polished, polite and refined. I loved the society dearly, and strove to improve by having such advantages; and memory holds enshrined in my heart the names of many ladies, of whom it gives me much happiness to think.

To tell you all that was of note in Montreal, would be to write a book about it. I will give you a few hints. Long, long ago, when the red man hunted, fished, and built his wigwam city there, they gave it the name of Hachelaga. The French, anxious to possess this beautiful domain, warred with the rightful owners, drove them out and built their own town there. They called it "Ville Maria:" afterwards Montreal, from Mount Royal. They built a wall around the town, but this did not keep it from falling into the hands of the English, under whose government it has grown to the city of note which it is. Mount Royal, back of the city, rises in majestic beauty, and, like a beacon light, can be seen from the country far around, to guide the stranger to the city. As you approach nearer, you are inspired with awe and reverence almost to a bowing posture, on viewing the many spires, the tall and elegant steeple of the English Church, and the massive grandeur of the French Cathedral, whose lofty towers reach into the sky, far above all else in the city. Or should you chance to enter it from the east on a bright sunny morning, you would exclaim, "A city of silver!" on beholding the reflection from the tin covered roofs, domes and spires.

The French, Scotch, English, and Americans are well represented in this city, besides a sprinkling other nations. Here can be seen all types of architecture, and as many ways of worshipping God. After the manner of the Jews, God is worshipped here in a Synagogue, which bears the type of Egyptian architecture; Saturday is their Sunday. The body of the building is occupied by the males; the gallery by the females. Opposite to the gallery is a very beautiful mahogany Ark, over which are placed the Ten Commandments, in Hebrew characters cut in white marble.

The grand, massive and magnificent French Cathedral presents the Gothic style of architecture; it is said to cover an acre of ground, and will seat ten thousand persons. Here the meek and lowly Nazarene is worshipped in a grand, showy, and imposing manner. The monster bell with others in the high towers above chimes out the call to matins and vespers—to high mass and low mass—to Christenings, marriages and funerals—to fate days and saint days —to feast days and fast days—and many kinds of Sundays. Many other Roman Catholic churches raise their pointed spires Heavenward, throughout the city. The French College, several Nunneries, Seminaries, and Friar's schools, all have chapels attached, where their occupants worship, and teach their own peculiar tenets.

All the Protestant sects and their secedings have elegant churches, and worship in their way, and hold to their tenets just as tenaciously as do the Romans —and why should they not?

Here too, worship the quiet, unpretending Unitarians, in a plain, inviting church, but to whom the hand of Christian fellowship is not extended, on account of their belief in a unity of the God-head, "Who shall judge between us?"

The houses are mostly of cut greyish lime-stone, massive, chaste and elegant; but there are many wooden houses, and marks of the old French town, besides squalid habitations, which fires will renovate.

Here come ships from the mighty ocean and distant seas, large river steamers, and a variety of smaller water craft. Here can be seen riches, honor, fashion, ease, and equipage ; also labor, poverty, toil, rags, and degradation.

The mountain is mostly covered with forest trees ; at its base, on gentle risings, flourish hundreds of acres of productive fruit trees—the apples are of the choicest and richest kind—and splendid gardens—and here are elegant retired dwellings. A ride round the mountain, seven miles, is a fascinating rarity to the stranger, who will be anxious to take a full view of the Governor's place as he passes it, and the Priest's farm, from whence can be seen scores of black attired priests and monks walking to and from the city. When on the top of the mountain the city is spread out down before you like a map, with its busy thousands; the masts of the shipping rise up from the blue waters of the majestic river; while beyond, as far as eye can see, can be seen a view of country dotted with habitations and church spires, and bounded by the distant blue mountains. The whole scenery is grand, rich, and enchanting. Late improvements and the mammoth bridge which spans the noble St. Lawrence, I cannot describe.

During most of the time of our residence in Montreal, my husband was engaged in teaching the Free School, or an academy of his own. I assisted him in the primary department what my health would allow. We boarded until the Fall of 1847; then we went to housekeeping. In the Winter a little daughter was made welcome, and blessed our home. Time rolled on; the mental wear of teaching brought my husband to the decision of dropping it, and choosing some business that would give him more stir in Heaven's pure air. I was willing to comply with his decision, but still I loved to dwell in the city,—its beautiful locality, its grand and picturesque scenery, the comfort and elegance of its homes, the refined society, and the very many attractions to kind and affectionate friends, all bound me with cords which were pleasant and agreeable to my nature,—but my path led out of the city.

Long after, I vainly hoped, and even prayed that some favorable turn in fortune would give me back a home in Montreal. And now, I often spend hours here in my lonely home, reviewing the many pleasant, happy seasons, and profitable too, that I spent there,—seasons of departed joys,

"Departed never to return."

In July, 1852, we left Montreal and came to St. Lawrence Co. In January, of 1853, a little son was given us, fondly welcomed as a lovely morn. He soon became the hope and pride of his parents' hearts. For two years my husband took book and paper agencies, which caused him to travel. I and my children boarded and visited during the time. In 1854, we went to live on the farm here in the town of Stockholm, from whence we started to meet you in St. Louis, as you already know.

My Dear Friend—As you also desire to know something of the early history of my dear, departed husband, I will begin by giving you a genealogy of the Colt family, as my husband traced and noted it from records kept in the family, previous to our emigrating to Kansas.

Sir John Colt, a Peer in England in Cromwell's day, headed his country's troops in the civil wars; had three horses killed under him; broke his sword in action, but replacing it gained the victory. From this circumstance came the Colts' coat of arms, emblematical of his exploits in this action. In the convulsions which followed, he lost his titles and estates, which were, however, restored to his son, Sir Peter Colt.

Sir Peter Colt, son of Sir John, remained Peer of the Realm. For the next four generations, I can only trace the family through the line that came to America.

John Colt, son of Sir Peter.

John Colt, son of John, and grandson of Sir Peter.

John Colt, son of John, and great-grandson of Sir Peter.

John Colt, son of John, and great great grandson of Sir Peter. He left Colchester, England, at the early age of eleven, and came to Hartford, Conn., in the early settlement of New England. Here he remained, an apprentice, until of age; he then removed to Windsor, Conn., where he married. From him alone sprung the Colt families in the U. S. A. His children were Abraham, John, Jabez and Joseph.

Abraham settled in Windsor, and had but a small family.

John, Jabez and Joseph, moved to Lyme, Conn. The last two had no issue. I am unable to state the year of John's death; it is said he reached the advanced age of 105.

John Colt, second son of John, born about 1657, settled in Lyme, Conn.; married Mary Lord; had two sons, Samuel and Benjamin; had several daughters, who married and raised respectable families. He died about 1750, aged 93.

Samuel had three children, one only of whom had issue; his eldest son, named after himself, has a large posterity. The father above mentioned read the Bible through in eight days, when above 80 years of age.

Benjamin Colt, eldest son of John, born at Lyme, Conn., about 1701, married Miriam Harris. He had ten children, seven sons and three daughters, viz: John, Joseph, Harris, Benjamin, Jonas, Jabez, Peter; and Mary, Sarah and Temperance. He died aged 56. John, Joseph and Harris lived and died in Lyme, Conn. Benjamin died in Hadley, Mass., 1780. Harris had four sons, Benjamin, Samuel, Elisha and Christopher. James lived and died at Pittsfield, Mass.; had ten sons. Jabez lived and died at Richmond, Mass.; had four sons. Peter lived and died at Patterson, N. J.; had two sons and three daughters. Mary married Dea. Thomas Giddings; Sarah married Joseph Harney; Temperance married Abner Lord. These ten children all raised families that have scattered all over the United States.

John Colt, eldest son of Benjamin, born in Lyme,

Ct., in 1725, died 1784, aged 59 years. He had three wives, Mary Lord, Mary Gardner, and Abigail Matson. By his first wife he had four children, viz: Esther, John, Miriam, and Amherst. By his second wife, Andrew, Gardner, and Benjamin; and by his third wife, William. Esther married Mathew Peck and raised a large family. John raised a family. Miriam married Joseph Burnam; had a family. All these eight children raised families but Andrew and Gardner, who were drowned at sea.

In 1853, I visited Dea. Wm. Colt, the only survivor of this family. He still lives in Lyme, Ct., on the old homestead that has been in the family for several generations; owns a large property; now lives with his second wife. Her name was Mary Marvin. Has had three children,—two daughters, one son; daughters both dead, never married. His son, William E., in 1853 was not married, and probably never will be; age 56 years, and lives with his father.

Dr. Amherst Colt, fourth child of John, was born at Lyme, Ct., July 27, 1759,—died at Auburn, N. H., Jan. 25, 1830. Was married to Miriam Giddings, Sept. 12, 1784. She was born April 22, 1762, at Hartford, Ct. By her he had the following children, John, born June 10, 1785, died in infancy; John Gardner, born July 15, 1787; Miriam, born April 18, 1789; Abigail, born March 6, 1791; William, born June 8, 1793; Aseneth, born May 1, 1795; Amherst, born May 17, 1797; Mary, born

March 9, 1799; Lydia, born March 9, 1799; Joseph, born Jan. 22, 1801, died in infancy. His wife, Miriam, died Oct. 29, 1805. He was again married, Sept. 23, 1806, to Mercy Giddings, widow of Jabez Giddings; her maiden name was Mercy Johnson. His second wife survived him several years, but raised no children. Dr. Amherst Colt studied the profession of medicine; was employed as surgeon several months in the American army of the Revolution. Near the close of the war emigrated to Lyme, N. H., which was then very new. Here he followed his profession for several years, but finally gave up his practice and turned his attention to farming, and for many years was an active and useful man in the town of Lyme. It was here that he raised his children, buried his wife and married again. He removed to Auburn, N. H., four or five years before his death, lived with his son William, and here died. His three sons and five daughters, who reached adult age, raised families.

John Gardner married Mary Smith, Jan. 20, 1813.* You know, my friend, that John G. Colt was my husband's father, and that he died in Kansas, Sept. 5, 1856.

My husband was born in Lyme, N. H., July 31, 1816. His parents had six children, of whom only

---

*Unfortunately, the branching of this family was not all given, so I will not give what I have. Wrote to the Colt relatives for it, but failed to get it.

one is living, Mary. They came to Parishville, St. Lawrence Co., N. Y., when my husband was but six years old. There he lived, working with his father on a farm, until he commenced his education; then he studied, taught school, and worked on the farm in the Summer season. He graduated at the St. Lawrence Academy of Potsdam, N. Y., in 1838, under Asa Brainerd, Principal at that time, as a teacher of all the English branches of education. He then intended to go South to teach; but a fond mother persuaded, and his sympathy being large, he put off the day, teaching Winters, and working the farm Summers, until he went to Montreal, in 1842, as you know; and you also know that he was married to another half in 1845. I could write pages delineating his many virtues; but as you saw him under very trying circumstances, and read him, it is not necessary. His scholarship has been noted by many as having been excellent,—and his memory, to me, is as sweet as the "nectar which the gods do sip."

Our Miriam Louisa Colt was born in Montreal, Dec. 22, 1847.

Our William H. Colt Jr., was born in Parishville, Jan. 21, 1853; died at Booneville, Mo., Sept. 14th, 1856, as you already know.

CHAPTER XIV.

"Only waiting till the shadows
    Are a little longer grown;
Only waiting till the glimmer
    Of the day's last beam is flown;
Till the night of Earth is faded
    From the heart once full of day;
Till the stars of Heaven are breaking
    Through the twilight soft and gray.

Only waiting till the reapers
    Have the last sheaf gathered home!
For the Summer time has faded,
    And the Autumn winds have come.
Quickly, reapers, gather quickly,
    The last ripe hours of my heart;
For the bloom of life is withered,
    And I hasten to depart.

Only waiting till the angels
    Open wide the mystic gate,
At whose feet I long have lingered,
    Weary, poor, and desolate;
Even now I hear the footsteps,
    And their voices far away;
If they call me I am waiting,
    Only waiting to obey.

Only waiting till the shadows
Are a little longer grown;
Only waiting till the glimmer
Of the day's last beam is flown;
Then from out the gathering darkness
Holy, deathless stars shall rise,
By whose light my soul shall gladly
Tread its pathway to the skies."

FEBRUARY 18TH, 1859.

MY DEAR MRS. VOORHEES:

I will answer your request as to how the world goes with me. You will remember I hinted to you my intention of improving my little home by having a white front fence, having my line fence made over, and then having my square lot set with maple trees all around—then have some nice shade trees set inside my front yard, together with rare shrubbery and flowers—thus making my rural retreat as pleasant, tasty, and neat as possible. But the times are so hard at the West that my interest cannot be paid, so my calculations cannot be carried out in doing the little business I had intended to keep us busy, and make us a livelihood—letting alone all ideas of ornamenting, except what we could do with our own hands.

In the Spring of 1858 I bought forty apple trees, (they are not yet paid for,) and had them set, thus commencing an orchard; had currant bushes taken up, that were growing in front of my house, and set in my garden, making two long thrifty rows; and a

few plum and cherry trees set near the house. I
and my Mema brought cherry trees, gooseberry bushes, and strawberry vines, two miles in our arms, and
set them. We re-set some peach and plum trees
that we brought from Michigan, in our trunks. We
went to the swamps for balsam and tamarack, to the
sugar bush for maples, and to the hills for sumac.
We set rose bushes, lilacs, various other shrubs and
vines, many of them presents from friends, and
sowed flower seeds. Methinks you ask, "Why! how
could you do it?" I will tell you. We would
choose small trees, such as we could handle, hoe off
the top dirt, leaves or moss, then take one root at a
time and loosen that, then another, and so on until
we got the tree. We would get five or six trees at
a time, lug them home, rest, then just at night dig
places for them, pour in water and sprinkle dirt
around the roots, and soon they would be made fast
in their new position. I would get so tired that I
would lay awake nights with lameness and pain, and
perhaps get a three days headache; but when I could
see the trees swell their buds, put forth leaves, and
grow larger, I felt paid for my toil.

I hired men to work by the day in cultivating my
land, we doing our garden work ourselves, which
kept us digging, weeding and hoeing, all the summer long. What I raised on my land would hardly
pay for the work of cultivating,—so it would not
make us a livelihood; and situated as I am, in the
country, cannot get work such as would help to sup-

17

port us, so I am obliged to turn my hand to anything that is within reach. Last fall I bought wool
and spun and prepared sock yarn, and these winter
evenings are spent in knitting sale socks, and in
meditation. I have had a boarder a few weeks, and
the pay will be a great help to me.

My brother's people across the way have been
sorely afflicted. Their only daughter, a beautiful
and lovely child of ten years, has sickened and died
with the scarlet fever. Their jewel has gone from
their household, and a shadow of deep mourning
broods over our pleasant hill.

> "Mother! could'st thou endure
>   To think thyself forgot
> By *her*, who was *thy life*, *thy air*,
>   The *sunbeam* of thy lot?
> Would'st thou not live in doubt and fear,
> If all thy bright hopes perished *here?*"

MARCH 21ST, 1860.

MY DEAR MRS. V——:

Pecuniary pressures are upon me as you shall
know. I have been obliged to get considerably into
debt to live, hoping all the time that my interest
money would be forthcoming, so that I could make
all straight, but it comes not yet. I was owing for
my cow, and for my wood, which is quite an item
even in this wooded country, with getting it all prepared for burning. I received some money last
spring that was due on a small mortgage, but felt

that I must pay it all to those whom I was owing, and in some way work out our living. I rented my lot, and with half of what was raised on it, some butter from my cow, a few eggs, the proceeds of a little domestic wine, a boarder awhile, and a little sewing that I have done, we have come along thus far with our necessities supplied.

My large debts, as I call them, were pressing upon me so heavily that last fall I went and mortgaged my little home here, and paid them. I have changed the place, but keep the pain. I felt that honor, that I had rather lose my home than to have others suffer losses by me. So what I am owing now is $300, all in one place. My interest, could I have it, would soon pay it and give us a livelihood besides. The saying is that "Misfortunes never come singly." Another that I have deemed misfortune is, that my brother, whom I came to live beside, has sold his farm, and on the first day of this month moved away; so I am left settled down in the country alone, where I would not have come but for the sake of living by my brother, and with my stake so firmly driven down, that it will take another adversity's upheaval to loosen it so that I could follow in their wake, even if I desired it. I have learned this lesson, that it will never do to follow friends around the world. It has proved unfortunate to me that I yearned to hover to the side of *consanguineous* friends—that I felt the want of a ladder, trellis, or oak, around which to twine for support. I must stand up like the lone weather-beaten pine on the plain, and take the winds and storms as I travel life's sandy desert, seeking shelter and protection from Him, who, when told that his brethren desired to speak with him, asked, "Who are my brethren?" Happy will be the time when the Christ principle of doing unto others as we would have them do unto us, shall be lived out—then my interest will be your interest, and your interest will be my interest—and by becoming, "My brother's keeper," or my sister's "keeper," we shall become our own keepers, and enrich ourselves far beyond the value of gold!

In the past year, I, with many others, have been wreathed in cypress and willow again. My most lovely sister Louisa, (Mrs. Briggs,) on the morning of the last Fourth of July plumed her wings of immortality and left this mortal sphere, leaving a husband and six children, besides numerous friends, to mourn.

A lovely niece of rare endowments in musical lore, has been suddenly removed from fond and doating parents, an adoring husband, and a large circle of friends.

Our friends leave us, and we say,

> "Alas! if it be so
>   That in the burial-urn
> The soul must garner up the love,
>   That once did in it burn,
> Better to know not of the worth
> Of true affection on this earth,

Better to live alone,
　　Unblessing and unblest,
Than thus to meet and mingle thought ;
　　Then from the immortal breast
Shut out the memory of the past,
Like day-beams from a forest vast.

Oh! no ; it cannot be !
　　Ye! the long-lost of years !
Mid all the changes of this life,
　　Its thousand joys and fears,
We love to think that round ye move,
Making an atmosphere of *love*."

You will be pleased to know that this sad heart of mine is often cheered with letters from Booneville, Mo.; and in summer-time they come laden with leaves from the rose, myrtle, and verbena, that my friends have planted on the graves of my loved ones, who are sleeping far away from me. *Leaves from off their graves.*

" Ye are faded all, and withered,
　　Sad reminders of the day"
When they bore them to the grave-yard,
　　And laid my darling ones away !

" Once I deemed it sad and gloomy,
　　In the 'city of the dead,'
Shuddered when its hallowed precincts
　　Echoed to my startled tread !"

" But I am no longer fearful,
　　When I rove" their " shades among ;"
Hold they " not my choicest" treasures,
　　" Heaven's best" gift, "my dearest" ones?

"Ye are faded, all, and withered—
   On" your "leaves, like summer rain,
Glisten now the pearly tear-drops,
   From a heart surcharged with pain."

"Ye have" grown "above" their bosoms,
   'Waved o'er mounds where I would grieve,
"From" their "dust ye've gathered" moisture—
   "How I love ye," withered leaves!'"

APRIL 18TH, 1861.

MY FRIEND MRS. V——:

Adversity, "stern rugged nurse!" still holds her sway over me. During the past year the first mortgage on the farm on which my security rested at the west has been going through the processs of foreclosing, which has given me considerable anxiety. I wrote to Mr. A. H. Byerly, the man that held the first mortgage, stating to him my circumstances, and that if there was anything in the farm that belonged to me I needed it. He wrote me that the amount of the first mortgage was about $3,200, and that the farm was well worth $5,000, and even more, and if I could send and pay the first, the farm would pay mine, and more. But I knew of no one that could assist me, so asked no one.

When the day of sale came, Mr. Byerly bid in the farm on the first mortgage—nothing was left for me. Thus you see, our laws will take the bread from the mouth of the widow and the fatherless, and lay it in the lap of the man worth more than his hundred thousands.   The weaker must submit to the stronger.

I learn that there is no sale for the village lots. Notwithstanding my dues come not—yet I *have been called upon to pay for the last nibble of grass my cow has taken in a generous man's pasture; though it has taken that which I would have held in pleasant remembrance of a promise I made in sunnier days.*

It often seems as though every thread of hope was cut off, leaving no way for us to obtain a livelihood. My physical health is not strong enough to enable me to labor for people; I could not stand it three days; neither can I send my child out to earn her bread, for I am so afflicted with my dreadful headaches and with their convulsive tendency, that it would not be safe for me to be left in my house alone. It is but little sewing I can get to do, for here in the country people generally do their own sewing— then it is the worst work for my poor head.   Were we situated in a town or village, I should try and do something at my old avocation, teaching, although my nerves are weak.   Last season hired my land cultivated, paying by the day, but when what I raised was stored in the fall, it would not have sold for enough to pay for the work.

I have learned not to want, and all I pray for, is bread to eat and wood to warm—apparel the plainest and cheapest, for we cannot desire superfluities, when we know not how that which serves to keep soul and body together is to be supplied. The past winter has seemed long, and loneliness has brooded around our little home,—the winds have blown cold and the snow has piled mountains high around, which we must needs dig through. Our "cruise of oil" has been almost drained—and almost the last stick of wood laid on the coals; yet my grateful thanks have ascended to Him who forgetteth not the sparrow, for my kind neighbors came to my relief, and have supplied me with a whole year's stock of wood.

My nephew who had my money, invested his all in said farm—he is now a poor man, with feeble health, and with a little family on his hands; still he has made an effort, and has just sent me fifteen dollars, which I know well how to appropriate. Should he be prospered, some time in the future I may hope for more.

We keep our a cow and a few hens, so that like the old swain,

> "In summer's heat and winter's cold"
> *We feed our "flock," and pen our "fold."*

Now, my dear friend, let me turn your attention from the foregoing adverse picture, and invite you to read a piece of my Mema's poetry.

THE WORLD'S A MYSTERY.

When first I woke to consciousness of living in this sphere,
My first thoughts were of wonder, how it was that I came here ;
The world and its busy throng they were but shadows to me—
And I turned away and thought " the world's a mystery."

I look'd around upon the world and on the bright blue sky ;
I thought of all the folks, "do they live, breathe, and think as I,"
Six sunny, sunny years pass'd o'er my head, years fraught with
    naught but joy,
For in the interim I had a brother—baby boy.

But clouds began to gather, and the distant storm to beat,
And soon it burst with violence around our pilgrim feet ;—
In a distant land they're laid, my father and my brother—
We are left lone in the world, me and my precious mother.

But still I love the world, and look with joy to the morrow,
Though poets and mis'thropes talk of " this vale of sorrow ;"
I make poetry at the wash-board and as I feed the cow—
And look around upon the world—it seems a mystery now.

I think of the ages past, and the ages yet to come,
And then it is I stop and wonder, "O, where is my home ?
Do I live in ages past, 'midst heroes, poets, and sages ?
Or am I a wand'rer from one of the future ages ?"

There's hope and ambition within, as seasons come and go,
And change from summer's heat to winter with its cold and
    snow ;
I make poetry at the wash-board and as I feed the cow—
'Tis true I am fourteen—but the world's a mystery now.

MIRIAM LOUISA COLT.

MAY, 1862.

DEAR MRS. V——:

You ask if I have as yet received anything purporting to come from my beloved husband in the Spirit Land. I answer in the affirmative. A little more than a year ago, I was feeling very low-spirited —almost in the "slough of despond," when in the secret chambers of my own heart, I made this request: "If my husband in his home of immortality takes cognizance of the passings of earth, and witnesses my desolation of heart, will he not through some medium commune with me?" It was only about two weeks after, when to my surprise I received the following message from a lady medium, enclosed in a letter:

MY DEAR MIRIAM—My dear wife—you are longing to hear from one who loves you yet. Dear wife, remember that I am with you—I long to comfort you—long to let you know how bright is the pure reward here for you. Have hope my love; skies may lower and all seem dark, but the day is dawning! Remember our little girl, she needs your care; watch over her carefully, and the angels will bless you. My boy is here—he sends love to mamma, and to Mema. May hope smile on you, my Miriam. Day after day I watch over you, and you cannot see me. I am near you—ever near you—always when affection calls. Good-bye, my dear, for this time.

From your husband, WM. H. COLT.

Last fall I sent a sealed letter to the same medium, in which were the following questions: What shall I do with my little home here? Can you read my thoughts? Do you know my troubles? When shall I come to you? Do you love me? Direct about Mema? What of my Willie? Do you see your father? In a short time I received the following answer, and my sealed letter unbroken:

DEAR WIFE—You ask for a test. I am not sure that one can be given whereby you will know me. Patience, O my dear. Do not give up your little all. Aid will come; my own help is always ready as far as I am able to give. Miriam, my own dear wife, it grieves me to see you doubt that I can see you. Sands of life are running short—you will soon join me—and, O, dear one, do not fear for a moment that eternity will be all dark. Poverty so afflicting is not known in this bright land. We love the same of ruin, the old loves of earth—we are so glad to bring glad tidings to them. You are tired, my Miriam. Your lamp is growing dim. There will be no more headaches nor heartaches on *this* side the river.* Will that comfort you? Rejoice! Willie is well cared for. Do not doubt for a moment that we are living yet. Father says, at times he revisits old scenes—he goes in, he says, and nobody

---

*He refers to the dream he had previous to our leaving Kansas, about fording the river.

says, "How d'ye do," or "Will you come in?"—and so he thinks nobody wants to see him. The old gentleman will have it so, and being rather obstinate, won't listen to my explanation.

My little girl—she is now grown almost out of knowledge, but I must not say out of remembrance. Perhaps the sitting, the studying so much may injure her more than you are aware of—her vocation is destined to be one of deeds, not such as you would have her perform, but are not the less useful, if she does right and keeps her system in good tune.

O, my dear, forget not that there is one who waits for you behind the veil. Keep up courage, and as regards worldly matters, could those better fitted by the place they occupy, give advice better than I, who stand apart, as it were? Yet I am willing to help you every way that seems needful to you. Always yours, my dear Miriam.

From your beloved

WM. H. COLT.

Last fall I was determined to sell my little home, and save what I could, so as not to have it sold on the mortgage, but could get no one to buy. After, I received the following through the same medium:

MY DEAR WIFE—Again I come on wings of love to thee. So you are going away from your home; I wish you could stay where you are. You are having many disappointments, but they will not always last

—and here you will find freedom from aught to vex or make afraid.

Now, my dear, let us reason together: you being just now in the "slough of despond," and tempted, and say to yourself,* "O! where is he that once would have protected me from the blasts of adversity? Can he imagine my forlorn condition wherever he is, and give to me of his advice?"

From my being incapable by the laws of nature and spirit of returning bodily and taking control of earth-born cares, fixing matters in my own way— which if all this could come to pass might not be after all just right—do not imagine for a moment that I am indifferent to your trials; for, Miriam, you ought to know that I am now where by the nature of things I am not so well fitted for acting in regard to pecuniary matters as I used to be. Still I am not at all desirous of your becoming a beggar while you dwell in the bad world,—and let me tell you again, this will not always last, though for a time you are obliged to ask for that which is your right, from those who ought by the ties of consanguinity and honor to see you protected—but the end, the end of sorrow is at hand. Your husband,

WM. H. COLT.

Again still later he says:

I would not have you discouraged or perplexed;

*These words have been spoken many times by myself.

there are bright days in store for you, my Miriam: you will then see clearly why so much is dark now; then how thankful you will be for the trouble you are undergoing, and rejoice we will all together, that the cloud has passed, leaviag our spirits more smilingly bright for the rain of sorrow that swept over them. * * * * Give my love to our daughter, and as for yourself, my Miriam, remember, I am "not lost—only gone before." Farewell. From your husband, WM. H. COLT.

Now my dear friend, you were acquainted with my beloved husband, so judge for yourself whether these breathings, purporting to come from him, seem to be like him. They have buoyed my spirit up when nigh sinking in despair. After reading them the following lines were suggested to my mind. *My husband's whisper*—

> Have dark sorrows round thee gathered,
>   Barbed with anguish fierce and sharp,
> All thy hopes and joys been smothered,
>   Pierced thee with a mourner's dart?
> Yet hope and trust, O do not fail!—
> I wait for thee behind the veil.
>
> Disappointment harsh and bitter
>   Has blown to thee on every breeze,
> Cutting off each true endeavor,
>   Causing thy light almost to freeze—
> Yet toil on, love, thou wilt prevail—
> I wait for thee behind the veil.

Thought oft you know not whence will come
  Your bread to eat or wood to warm;
His store is full, for all there's some—
  Be troubled not by winter's storm;
Though dark the days that may assail—
I wait for thee behind the veil.

Remember now, my own dear wife,
  With patience all thy ills endure;
Add lustre to thy crown of Life—
  Glory an eternal weight insure;
Though laden with the widow's wail—
I wait for thee behind the veil.

"Not lost," I'm "only gone before"
  Into my Father's Mansion, where
There's covert when life's storms are o'er—
  'Tis there I'll meet you love, 'tis there;
Your sands of life soon, soon will fail—
I wait for thee behind the veil.

Do you wonder, my friend, that when I have thought of this war that is scourging our land— brother warring with brother—the suffering it produces—the keen sorrow and anguish it is sending to almost every hearthstone, that I have congratulated myself that my husband and son are safely moored far beyond the dismal cannon's roar and the bloody carnage of the battle-field?

When will earth's inhabitants "learn war no more?" When that new commandment is lived up to, "*that ye love one another.*"

You ask, "How do you like your neighbors?" I

will tell you. The parents of the interesting family who purchased my brother's farm across the way, were once from the *Green Isle* of the ocean. Mr. Hayes is a quiet, pleasant, unassuming man, who brings up his family in the way they should go; and from the least to the greatest of eight boys, nothing but propriety, good breeding and marks of perfect gentlemen are to be seen. Mrs. Hayes is a true, whole-souled, and noble woman; and Mary, the only daughter, is a picture of health, youth, and beauty, and a model of female loveliness. She is an agreeable and useful associate for Mema, and the whole family are very kind indeed to us.

For the five long years that I have lived here almost a recluse, shut out from society, I am indebted to my friends, Mr. and Mrs. Mathews, who live under the hill, for my peeps out into the big world. They, by their kindness in my desolation, have proved themselves worthy the name of brother and sister; but I do think, now after the confinement through the past howling winter, that should I visit any public place, even to church, there might be danger of my going bare-footed, and of my standing in the doorway to make my obeisance to the audience. My neighbors are all so kind that I often think I could not live without them.

I am trying to fit my Mema to make her own way in the world, by having her prepare herself for teaching. She has attended the district school since we have lived here—and in fact, she never attended

school until we came here. Last fall, by the assistance of friends, I was enabled to send her to a select
school kept two miles away; she walked back and
forth each day, staying out only two days during the
term of twelve weeks. She has a pretty good knowledge of the elementary branches, geography, grammar and arithmetic; and has studied algebra,
McElligott's Analytical Manual, ancient and mod-
ern history, philosophy and physiology, and loves to
read. In the time of flowers her botany, Breck's
Book of Flowers, and the Poetry of Flowers, are
often perused, giving her much pleasure. Could
she have the advantage, she would make a scholar;
she however improves her time at home, and has my
assistance.

The poultry business, like everything else I have
undertaken, has proved a failure; not that it could
not be made as profitable as keeping cows, for I have
done enough at it to know that it could, if a person
could take advantage of the times in getting in
food for them when it could be got at the lowest
price, and in marketing their own eggs and chickens; but when manacled it is hard to labor and have
it tell; it is also profitless to labor at arms length.
Mema, however, has taken much pleasure in looking
after the hens, petting the chickens, and gathering
the eggs. In our hen park, empires and kingdoms
have risen and gone to decay; thrones have been
abdicated and kingdoms usurped; renowned person-
ages have lived and died or been guillotined. Darius,
Ninus, Alexander the Great, Julius Cæsar, Lady

Jane Grey, Mary Queen of Scots, Queen Elizabeth, Louis Fourteenth, Maria Antoinette, Napoleon, Victoria, Prince Albert, and the Prince of Wales, have all figured here in hen-dom. Our number of hens is only eight now; it consists of one pair of white-faced black Spanish, that are known by the name 'of Ferdinand and Isabella—grandma'am Rosa Bramah, the only one left of the Michigan emigrants, now five years old, and enjoying a quiet life —and five peasants.

We still keep our noble cow dairy, and are raising her cow baby, Lily, which is a perfect fac simile of its mother. The above mentioned, and Foxy Johnny, (our red cat,) are all that we have the care of, that breathe the breath of life.

You would know, if I said no more, that poverty is still gaping upon us; but you know that I am bound to tell the whole story—just how life goes with me. My nephew is still in poor health, but is doing what his health will permit, at teaching among the Indians up Lake Superior; consequently he has no money for me. On account of the rainy season last year, I had nothing to speak of raised on my lot excepting hay for my cow. I have had to buy potatoes. I committed the sin of trafficking again in ardent spirits, in the shape of a little currant wine, that I made from currants picked from my own bushes. But when fall came, we had not the wherewith to procure our necessities through the cold winter. But HE who feedeth the ravens, has fed, warmed and clothed me and my child; thereby keeping us from the streets and the county house, through the kindness and benevolence of my much esteemed Montreal friends. My gratitude to God and to them cannot be measured by a whole catalogue of big-sounding words,—their reward is with them for drying the tears of the widow, and comforting the fatherless. I have given my bread freely to all who have come to partake with me, and I am glad that I still have something "*when somebody comes.*"

Notwithstanding our little home is under a mortgage, (which by the way runs out next fall,) we have tried to improve it all we could with our own hands; so from year to year we have added to our fruit and shade trees. Last spring we set twenty small apple-trees, and those that had been set three years, in the fall yielded four apples. This year we were expecting a full supply from them, but the deep snows of the past winter produced such a famine among the mice that they were driven to subsist on the bark of trees; consequently when the snow melted away, we found that the bark from the trunks of our apple trees had been gnawed off one-half yard up. I bandaged them with cloths, applying a plaster from the cow stable, and now the most of them look as though they would live.

Our shade trees, shrubbery, and climbing vines are growing finely. We can almost describe our home—(can when the trees and vines grow a little more,) thus—

" 'Tis a cottage, small and fair,
As a cloud in summer air.
White it rises 'mid the leaves,
Woodbines clamber o'er its eaves,
And the honey-suckle falls
Pendant, on its silent walls."

Mema had last year fifty kinds of flowers, which gave us much pleasure and knowledge; she will have more this year. I think we shall have a good supply of plums, cherries, currants, strawberries and raspberries. One of our peach trees still survives, and our pear trees, quince trees, and grape vines are thriving.

I rejoice in the return of green fields and woods, and the buds and flowers of spring, and can, with the little birds,

"Praise God, from whom all blessings flow."

My prayer to Heaven is, that I may profit by past experiences, and have grace to bear all the remaining reverses that may come in my pathway. Until more transpires of note,—ADIEU.

APPENDIX.

VEGETARIAN SETTLEMENT COMPANY.

THE many applications from all parts of the continent, and from Europe, which we are continually receiving relative to the character and operations of this Company, render it imperative that we furnish facts in a form which, we trust, will be easily understood and appreciated. This will be regarded as a reply to the general inquiries made on the subject.

ORIGIN.

The Octagon plan of settlement was originated by HENRY S. CLUBB, of New York City, in 1855. It was first adopted by the Vegetarian Settlement Company, which has made rapid and unexpected progress, having already a sufficient number of members to commence a CITY containing an area of sixteen square miles, a site for which has been selected on the banks of the Neosho River, Kansas Territory. The capital of this Company in February, 1856, amounted to over $33,000, and the private capital of members to over $100,000.

The Octagon Settlement Company is the second to adopt the Octagon plan, and although it commenced subscription to stock only in February, 1856, by the end of that month it numbered sufficient members to start one Octagon village of four miles square of area, and its shareholders are daily increasing, so that it is probable that before the end of the winter sufficient members will be secured to form a city of equal size to that of the Vegetarian Company.

THE SITE.

The site selected for the Vegetarian City, is on the Neosho River, between latitude 38°, and the boundary line of the Osage Indian lands, and between 18° and 19° longitude west from Washington. It is on the opposite side of the river to the settlement of the Octagon Settlement Company. The river at this part is very rapid, and for ten months in the year the water is sufficiently abundant to make it serviceable for mill-power. It is free from any bad taste, and is very soft. There is a sufficient amount of timber to serve the purposes of settlers until additional timber can be grown. Coal, Limestone, and Sandstone, suitable for grindstones, &c., and abundant springs of pure water, are interspersed throughout a fine rolling prairie, and the land comprises excellent vegetable mould, loam, &c., to a great depth, with a gravelly, and in some instances, rocky substratum. The limestone is well adapted for building, being at first easily cut, and becoming very hard by exposure. It will be seen by reference to the map of *American Railway Guide*, that a Pacific Railroad is projected, which will cross the Neosho River a little below the spot above indicated. The scenery is very beautiful, and the surface undulating, like the waves of the ocean subsiding after a storm. The banks of the river are from fifteen to thirty feet high, and there are several perennial streams adapted for water-power, emptying themselves into the river near this site.

In a work entitled *Kansas and Nebraska*, by JOSEPH H. MOF-FETTE, late of Governor Stevens' Overland Expedition, we find the following description of the Neosho River:

"The Neosho River rises in about latitude 38 deg. 30 min., and flows about 150 miles through a highly productive, beautiful, and well-timbered country. Its direction is about southeast to the State line of Missouri, the bluffs, as you approach which, become more elevated and picturesque : it has a bold, rapid current, over a rocky bottom, and upon its tributaries (which are numerous) water-power to any extent may be obtained. The wild pea grows spontaneously in its valley, and upon one of its tributaries an immense deposit of lead has been discovered. The mine is now being worked successfully; the ore is shipped in flat-boats down the Neosho and Arkansas rivers to Fort Smith."

The following account of this river, from recent explorations, will be found interesting: 'Near the southeast corner of the territory, the Neosho (clear or pure) River, descending from the southwest, passes out of the territory on its southern line. The Neosho is a bold, rapid, rocky stream, water clear, unfit for navigation, but affording admirable water-power. The bottom lands along its tributaries are of the finest description, and covered with excellent timber, and in much greater quantities than in the Kansas Valley. The bottom lands on the lower part of the Neosh yield enormous crops of corn, and every production common to the latitude of 37°, and have been known on rare occasions to produce two full crops of corn within the year. [*Vide* Report of Union Mission.] The uplands in this valley are generally of a lighter character, and well adapted to the growth of the smaller grains. Lead ore and stone coal are found upon its tributaries, and the springs and streams are pure and lasting. Council Grove is located upon the main branch of this river, only a few miles from Kansas river. Emigrants desiring to explore or settle in this valley, should pursue the Santa Fe road to Council Grove, and there ascend or descend the valley, as they may choose. With the surpassing beauty of scenery, broad and fertile bottom lands, beautiful timber, perennial springs, mild and pleasant climate of this valley, they cannot fail to be pleased. As a stock-grazing country this is among the most desirable parts of the territory.'"

In MAX GREENE's *Kanzas Region*, the following description appears:

"Throughout the Osage country there are scenes of romantic loveliness; and some even bordering on the picturesque. In tranquil summer-time, it has the plain yet dreamy beauty of the

Flemish landscape. Over all, a Sabbath serenity is diffused; and grassy knoll and leafy wood are embathed in a soft and subdued lustre, which is indescribably soothing, and inspires holiest impulses. Remembrances come to me now, of one full August of soul-felt enjoyment, because it was a life so novel and so free, every evening of which my blanket was spread upon one or the other of its tufted hill-tops. Then, goldenly, the sun would go down, and crimson bannerets of clouds would follow in his royal wake. The tall grass would wave beneath the zephyr stealing up, like a pet bird of stillest wing, from the twilight reaches of the dell beneath."

Such are the descriptions given of the country in which this City is situated, by men who could have no interest in a Company which has been originated since these extracts were written. The location of an enterprising company in such a locality, cannot fail to produce a successful settlement. A Hydropathic Establishment, an Agricultural College, a Scientific Institute, a Museum of Curiosities and Mechanic Arts, and Common Schools, will be among the first Institutions of the new settlement. The manufacture of lumber, agricultural implements and machinery, portable houses for new settlers, the preparation of provisions for market, woollen goods, &c., will be among the first manufacturing operations; while the development of the natural resources of the country, its mineral wealth, and its vast agricultural riches, will constitute the main occupation of the settlers. No one who examines the description of the country above given, and then the list of persons with their trades and occupations, can fail to see that the prospects of forming a city of considerable wealth and importance are very good, and consequently, as every shareholder participates in the profi s produced by the rise in the value of property, every shareholder may reasonably anticipate a handsome return for capital and labor invested.

OCTAGON PLAN OF SETTLEMENT,

Represents the disposition of four square miles of land.

AREA OF PLAN.	ACRES.
16 farms, 102 acres each, - - - - -	1632
16 equal triangular divisions of central octagon, to be held in common, 13 acres to each, - - - -	208
4 corners, to be held in common, 146 acres each, or $36\frac{1}{4}$ acres to each farm, - - - - - -	584
8 roads, 85 chains long, 10 square chains to the acre, -	136
160 acres, located by each one of the 16 persons, -	2560

In the farm here contemplated, the advantages to new settlers would be as follows :

1. Every settler would *live in a village*, and at the same time be in the best possible situation on his farm—between pasture land in front, and arable land in the rear of his dwelling,

2. Every settler would enjoy the mutual aid and protection of the other settlers, affording the best opportunity for co-operation in store, implements, teams, machinery and sales.

3. Educational advantages could be secured to children, the school-house in the centre, being within a quarter of a mile of all the farm-houses. The situation of the school-house is peculiarly healthy, with plenty of space for play grounds, and pure air around the building.

4. The intellectual advantages to settlers are worthy of consideration, as by assembling together frequently in the central building, for the discussion of agricultural, physiological, mechanical, and other sciences, politics, theology, and morals, the greatest amount of intelligence will be kept active, and the dullness and monotony, often incident to country life, avoided.

5. The social habits of improvement occasioned by such proximity, must be evident. In isolation, men become indifferent to the refinements of civilized society, and sometimes sink into barbarism ; but living in proximity in this way, will cause emulation to excel in the arts of domestic and social life, and in the elevating influences of mental and moral cultivation.

6. The pecuniary advantages of this plan arise from the fact

that the formation of a village always increases the value of the land all around. Now, these first sixteen settlers, if they erected their houses in various points of the territory, or even in various parts of these four sections of land, without any regard to plan, could only raise the value to that of *farm land*, but by settling in this form, the idea of a village or town is immediately suggested. Land which can be obtained at $1,25 per acre, as soon as settled on this plan, becomes eligible for a town site, and those of the settlers who choose, may dispose of portions of their land for building purposes. Five dollars per acre could be obtained from the very first commencement of such a village, and it would be cheap at that price.

To show the plan of dividing the farms, so as to give an idea of how all the farms may ultimately become settled as for town or city wards, one farm is divided into eight squares or blocks, forming also eight streets, from one avenue to the other. These squares, although varying in size, will probably be of about an equal value, owing to their proximity to the centre decreasing with their increase in size. As shown by the farm plan, each of these squares is divisible into twenty lots, which vary from 90 feet square and 70 feet wide by 150 deep, to about an acre and a half, the principle of increase in size as equivalent to increase of distance from the centre being observed throughout.

7. The plan contemplated by the company embraces an area of four of these octagon villages, forming a city of sixteen square miles, with a square in the centre of 584 acres, to be appropriated to an agricultural college and model-farm, to be cultivated by the students, who will pay for their education by their labor. Large plans of the city from actual surveys, will be published in the ensuing season 1856, and can be had on application to the agents, or officers of the company.

In connection with this plan of settlement, a plan of co-operation has been established, which secures the following advantages:

1. By the payment of $1 as entrance fee, and 10 cents instalment on each $5 share, not less than 20 nor more than 240 shares, each member becomes entitled to as many city lots as he takes shares in the company, and can take possession of them as soon after the payment of such instalment as he may think proper.

2. The industrious man or woman, who has no more money than the amount of the first payment and cost of reaching the settlement, may pay all further assessments on shares by their labor for the Company, at fair remunerative wages.

3. The land will cost, to each settler, only the Government price of $1 25 per acre, which will be paid to Government by the Company, or City Corporation. All the money subscribed above that amount, being $3 75 per share or per acre, (if the full $5 per share should ever be required,) would be used by the Company for provisions, the construction of streets, public schools, mills, stores, &c. ; and whatever profits might arise from the working of mills, or the sale of provisions, will be equally divided between the shareholders, according to the number of shares held by each ; so that every shareholder will enjoy equally the benefit of improvements effected.

4. Every shareholder, by the aid of co-operation, will be enabled to commence operations on his farm on the best plans, because the Company will secure the implements, teams, &c., which persons without capital could not obtain, especially in isolated positions. The advantages of farming with proper facilities, and without them, make all the difference between success and failure.

5. Every shareholder possesses, in his own right and title, the land included in his or her lots corresponding to his or her shares. All premiums paid for preference in selection of lots will, according to Art. IX. of Constitution, go into the common fund, and diminish the assessments required for carrying on the operations of the Company ; so that persons who have no preference in choice receive the benefit of the payments of those

who have the preference, by being relieved of payments in the form of assessment.

6. Every member will be secure against the impositions of speculators, as the provisions of the Company will be sold at prices agreed upon by members, or subject to their control.

7. Every member will reap the full reward of his or her own industry, and will not be subjected to loss by the indolence or indifference of other members, the co-operative principle being adopted so far as to *promote*, and not to supersede, individual enterprise, and officers being subject to the election of its members.

8. The settlement will be free from the evils of intemperance, flesh-eating, &c., as every member of the Company agrees to abstain from intoxicating liquors and the flesh of animals, during his or her residence in the settlement. The Octagon Settlement Company adopts merely the Temperance principle.

9. The co-operation of members will be directed to aiding each other in manufacturing, mining, and agricultural enterprises.

10. The issue of scrip, exchangeable, under certain regulations, for lumber, provisions, dry goods, &c., with the Company, will form a medium of exchange which will greatly facilitate all the dealings of members with each other and the Company.

We have thus endeavored to demonstrate the several features of this enterprise. We have shown, first, the advantages of the location selected; secondly, the peculiar benefits of the octagon plan of settlement; and, thirdly, the advantages of the system of co-operation adopted by the Company. To these may be added the political and patriotic motive, which should be sufficient to induce every friend of freedom and humanity to aid in this effort to establish free and civilizing institutions in one of the fairest and most fertile regions of the globe.

PROGRAMME OF ROUTES.

The first settlers proceed—

	Miles.
From St. Louis to Batesville, Mo., (steamer)............300	
" Batesville to Fort Scott, (teams).................. 20	
" Fort Scott to the settlement, (teams)............... 30	
	350

The Steamer leaves St. Louis for this route on 2d of April, 1856.

Persons arriving in St. Louis too late for the steamer, will inquire of Mr. SLATER, 19 Levee.

Those who wish to join the next party, will apply to the agents of the Company.

1. Every member to bring along as little baggage as possible, especially if the distance by railroad be great, as the cost of freight is greater in such cases than the value of the articles. Freight from New York to St. Louis, is from $1 75 to $3 00 per 100 lbs. St. Louis is the place to make purchases.

2. Any member who is referred to another member to correspond with such member previous to starting, stating the precise time he or she will start, &c.

3. Persons living in the Eastern States, coming after the Ohio river is open for navigation (which may be the middle of March,) can correspond with WALTER & CAMPBELL, Room 24, No. 229 Broadway, New York city, as to whether any cheaper fares than those indicated [see *ADAMS*] have been secured. Enclose stamps for reply when by letter. Persons passing through New York City can call on Messrs. W. & C., and they will afford them polite attention and give information.

4. Each member to start as nearly as possible according to the following arrangement :

[The following are the names of those who went to Kansas. Many others went whose names are not noted :]

ADAMS, James, Rahway, N. J., *Blacksmith,* wife and one
son. To leave New York City, Wednesday, March 12th, at
6 p. m. When in St. Louis, inquire of Mr. B. SLATER, 19
Levee, for the Secretary.

ADAMS, Archibald, Rushford, N. Y.

BAGNALL, Thomas, Mercer, Pa., *Farmer*, wife and three children. To come either by teams and caravan to St. Louis, or *via* Ohio and Penn. R.R., from Pittsburgh. See *ADAMS*.

BARKER, Anna M., New York City, *Widow*. See *AD-AMS*.

BLACKBURN, D. F., Hampshire, Tenn., *Printer*, wife and three children. By team *via* Springfield, Missouri, to Fort Scott.

BROADBENT, John, Bluff City Mills, Memphis, Tenn., two sons, *Woolen Manufacturer*. See *BLACKBURN*.

BUXTON, Josiah, Pontiac, Oakland Co., Mich., *Farmer*. To start with SAMUEL SREWART's party, Lafayette. *Via* Michigan City. See *STEWART, Samuel*.

CLUBB, Henry S., N. Y. City, *Secretary, Jourualist*, wife. To start Saturday, March 8th, *via* Philadelphia, Pittsburgh, and Cincinnati, where he will stay two days, then to St. Louis, where he will stay probably ten days, Address at St. Louis, care of B. SLATER, 19 Levee. After April 2nd, Fort Scott, K. T.

COLT, Wm. H., Hopkinton, N. Y. *Farmer*, wife and two children. To St. Louis, by March 25. See *SOBER*.

COSGROVE, John, West Point, N. Y., *Gardener*. See *ADAMS*.

DAVIS, David, Pittsburgh, *Merchant*. See *ADAMS* for routes, and start *via* Ohio River.

HARDING, Wm. B., 122 W. 34th Street, N. Y. City, wife, *Builder*. See *ADAMS*.

HERRIMAN, Angus A., Greenbush, Wis., wife, *Farmer*. See *SMITH, J. H.*

HOBBS, Geo., Mt. Vernon, Ohio, *Nurseryman*, wife and brother-in-law. To come *via* Indianapolis. See *ADAMS* and *CLUBB*.

LAYARD, J. C., Mitchell's Map Office, cor. 5th and Chestnut si., Philadelphia, *Merchant*. See ADAMS.

McLAURIN, John, Treasurer, Water Cure Physician. See CLUBB.

ROOT, George H., Boonton, N. Y., *Farmer.* See ADAMS.

SOBER, Albert J., Salem, Washtenaw Có., Mich., *Farmer,* 1 brother. See BUXTON and SMITH, J. H.

SOMERVILLE, Wm., Lonsdale, R. I., *Weaver,* wife and daughter. Ohio River from Pittsburgh. See ADAMS, Jas.

STEWART, Samuel, Lafayette, Ind., *Farmer.* To form a party about March 1st, and come by teams and wagons to St. Louis. See CLUBB.

STEWART, Watson, Lafayette, Ind., *Stonecutter,* wife, mother-in-law, and two children. To come *via* St. Louis. See CLUBB.

VOORHEES, Henry, Pontiac, Mich., W., *Farmer.* See BUXTON.

WHEELER, Lyman, Oxford, Butler Co. Ohio, *Farmer.* See CLUBB and ADAMS.

YOUNG, Stephen, Poplar Ridge, wife and child, *Cabinetmaker.* *Via* Cincinnati. See CLUBB.

CONSTITUTION.

WHEREAS, the practice of Vegetarian diet is best adapted to the development of the highest and noblest principles of human nature, and the use of the flesh of animals as food tends to the physical, moral, and intellectual injury of mankind, and it is desirable that those persons who believe in the Vegetarian principle should have every opportunity to live in accordance therewith, and should unite in the formation of a company for the permanent establishment in some portion of this country, of a home where the slaughter of animals for food shall be prohibited, and where the principle of the Vegetarian diet can be fairly and fully tested, so as to more fully demonstrate its advantages; therefore,

RESOLVED, That we, the undersigned, do hereby agree to form ourselves into a Vegetarian Settlement Company, and to abide by the following constitution:

ARTICLE I.—OBJECT.

1. The establishment, in the centre of the United States, of permanent homes for Vegetarians, where all the appliances for the production of their favorite articles of diet, fruits and farinaceous productions are at hand; namely, rich soil, salubrious and healthful climate, pure water, &c.

The concerted action of Vegetarians so associated, to be used for the establishment of a system of direct dealing, supplying the productions of the soil of the best quality direct from the producers to the consumers, without the enormous profits of speculators and retailers coming between these respective parties.

3. The dissemination of practical Vegetarian information, in connection with the supply of the articles of Vegetarian diet.

4. The calling public attention to the subject of Vegetarian diet in a way no mere theoretic movement in the form of lectures or publications ever can be expected to accomplish.

ARTICLE II.—PRINCIPLE.

The Company shall be conducted on the Mutual Joint Stock principle, for the equal benefit of all the members, and to protect each other from the imposition of speculators and monopolists; by raising sufficient funds to start with efficient machinery, implements, and provisions.

ARTICLE III.—OFFICERS.

The officers shall consist of a President, Secretary, and Treasurer, *pro tem*, who shall constitute a Board of Directors, and have entire control of the movements of the Company until a majority of the members shall meet and organize; at which time the permanent officers of the Company shall be elected, whose duty it will be to act under the direction of regular meetings, and to direct all affairs of the Company. The officers to receive such compensation for their services, by salary or otherwise, as the regular meetings of the shareholders shall decide.

ARTICLE IV.—QUALIFICATION OF MEMBERS.

Persons of good moral character, who shall be approved by the Board of Directors, whether male or female, and who are not slaveholders, may become members of the Company, on paying one dollar entrance fee, and an instalment of ten cents per share on not less than twenty shares. Each member may subsequently purchase additional shares. No member, however, shall be allowed to hold more than two hundred and forty shares at any one time. Each person, on becoming a member, must agree to sign the following declaration on entering the settlement:

I, —————————, do voluntarily agree to abstain from all intoxicating liquors as beverages, from tobacco in every form, and from the flesh of animals; to promote social, moral, and political freedom; to maintain the observance of all good and righteous laws, and to otherwise conform to the rules adopted by a majority of the Vegetarian Settlement Company.

ARTICLE V,—CAPITAL.

The capital stock of the Company shall consist of shares of five dollars each, equal in number to the acres of land located by the Company, and payable by members in money—or labor, if required—within four years; payable in such instalments as the Directors may call for. Any money or labor paid in advance of calls, shall be regarded as loans to the Company, and shall be paid for at the rate of one per cent. per month.

ARTICLE VI.—TRANSFER OF SHARES.

In case a member shall fail to keep up payments for the full amount of his shares according to the calls of the Directors or Company, the shares of such member shall be put up one by one at auction, until a sufficient amount is realized to secure the payment of the demands of the Company, with interest at the rate of one per cent. per month, and expenses of such sale; three months notice of such sale being previously given to such defaulter. Any member may sell his or her shares, provided the person to whom such sale is to be made, is approved of by the Board of Directors or the agent they may appoint for such purpose. The deed for conveying shares shall not be valid unless signed by the Directors or their duly appointed agent, as being recorded in the books of the Company.

ARTICLE VII.—ELECTION AND VOTING.

Each member shall have as many votes as shares he or she

may hold in the Company, on all questions involving the appropriation of funds, but on all other questions each member shall have only one vote. Absent members may vote by their duly authorized agents by proxy. Questions involving a change in the Constitution of the Company, must be submitted to every member, whether resident in the settlement of the Company or otherwise, and the vote of a majority of such members as vote shall decide such questions.

ARTICLE VIII.—SETTLEMENTS.

Whenever sufficient persons shall have paid the instalments of ten cents per share, it shall be the duty of the Directors or their agents to cause a suitable site of land to be surveyed on the Octagon plan, and provide such machinery, provisions, &c., as they may deem necessary for the success of the enterprise for which they shall make a call or assessment upon the said shareholders proportionate to the requirements of the settlement. That such of said shareholders as can, conveniently to themselves, shall be expected to co-operate with the Company in preparing the settlement, for which they shall receive compensation according to the value of their services, at the prices of such labor in the territory, or as fixed by the majority of members in such settlement, in money, scrip, or receipts for instalments on the shares subscribed for by each. The members living at the settlement to make their own by-laws and regulations, in accordance with the drovisions of this Constitution. Chattel-slavery shall not ba tolerated within the limits of the settlement.

ARTICLE IX.—DISPOSITION OF LOTS.

The plan of each settlement shall be divided into lots, according to the number of acres. The selection of lots shall be as follows: Each enclosure of about one hundred and sixty lots shall be put up at auction among the members of the Company. Those who paid the first instalment by the time fixed upon by the Directors, have the preference in selection without the competition of those who subsequently pay the same, and the highest bidder shall have the right of possession to as many lots as shall correspond to the shares for which he shall have so previously subscribed ten cents per share. The remaining lots of said enclosure, should there be any, and the remaining enclosures shall be put up in the same way. If paid within a month, the amount bid shall be subject to six per cent. discount; if not within that period, it shall be subject to one per cent. per month interest until paid.

ARTICLE X.—CURRENCY.

The scrip or receipt for money or labor held by each member, shall be exchangeable for provisions, lumber and other property of the Company, according to the amount of stock or supply on hand. The prices of provisions, lumber, etc., to be fixed by the Directors, or under the direction of a regular meeting of the members of the settlement. But the said scrip cannot be accepted for the purchase of the lands of the Company, except from recognized and duly recorded members thereof, their assigns, heirs, or administrators.

ARTICLE XI.—PURCHASE AND TRANSFER OF LANDS.

The Directors as Trustees on behalf of the Company, shall procure titles to the lands settled by the members thereof, and convey the separate lots or parcels of land, with all the rights and privileges therewith connected, one lot for every paid-up share in the Company, on the presentation at the office of the Company of scrip proving the payments for such shares. *Provided*, however, the land on which the Company shall settle be not, at the time of settlement, in the market, each member who is eligible shall procure pre-emption claims according to statute. This Company in such cases to aid its members in making the necessary payments for their lands, when required by government to purchase their pre-empted lands. Nothing in this Constitution shall be construed as at variance with the pre-emption laws of the United States. At the end of four years from the first commencement of each settlement, or sooner if desired by a majority of members, there shall be a general making up of the accounts of the settlement; all arrearages of members must be paid or collected by the process prescribed in Article VI., after three months' notice; the property of the Company shall be sold by auction; and whatever profits may have been realized, after paying all expenses connected with such settlement, shall be equally divided among the shareholders or proprietors of the same, according to the amount of shares held by each.

ARTICLE XII.—MEETINGS.

There shall be a semi-annual business meeting of the Company after the settlement shall have commenced, on the second Tuesday of every January and the second Tuesday in July, at which time the reports of the officers having charge of the affairs of the Company shall be present, and the officers for the succeeding year shall be elected at the January meeting by ballot. Special meetings may be held at any time on the call of one or more Directors, or at the request of six shareholders. A majority of the members residing at the time in the settlement to constitute a quorum. All the meetings to be conducted according to established parlimentary usage, subject to such modification and by laws as may be decided upon by such meetings.

ARTICLE XIII.—LIABILITIES.

No individual member of the Company shall be liable for any debt contracted by the Company or its officers.

ARTICLE XIV.—ARBITRATION.

All disputes between members and each other, or the Directors, shall be settled by arbitration.

----------------------------18----

I,-- agree

APPENDIX.

to abide by the provisions of this Constitution, to the best of my ability, and in testimony thereof, I hereby attach my name.

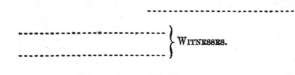

$\left.\begin{array}{c} \text{-----------------------------} \\ \text{-----------------------------} \\ \text{-----------------------------} \end{array}\right\}$ WITNESSES.

One copy to be retained by the member, and the other to be retained by the Secretary with signature. Those members who signed the first edition of the Constitution will, if they approve of the additions now made, (Articles XIII and XIV,) please to sign this, and return it to the Secretary without delay.